Khanjar
Hanpattar 12,500 ft

L A H H O U L

Miyar River

Udaipur

Chandrabhaga River

Baralacha Pass 16,000 ft

Chobia Pass 16,400 ft

Kuldeo Temple

Bhaga River

KEYLANG

Kugti

adsar

Kugti Pass 16,000 ft

GADDERAN I N

Kailash 18,564 ft

O

Barabangahal

Bajoli

Jalsu Pass 11,200 ft

D H A R

RNAGAR

Jathingri

Uhl River

Dulchi Pass 7,500 ft

KULU

KOKSAR

Murhi
Rothang
Kothi 13,200 ft

Chandra River

K U L U

MANALI

Hampta Pass 14,300 ft

A L

Beas River

Parbati River

Larji

MANDI

BILASPUR
SIMLA

00032519- I

Author's Route ··········

0   20 km

OVER THE HIGH PASSES

OVER
THE HIGH PASSES

A Year in the Himalayas
with the Migratory Gaddi Shepherds

Christina Noble

COLLINS
8 Grafton Street, London W1
1987

William Collins Sons and Co. Ltd
London · Glasgow · Sydney · Auckland
Toronto · Johannesburg

BRITISH LIBRARY CATALOGUING IN PUBLICATION DATA

Noble, Christina
  Over the high passes: a year in the
  Himalayas.
  1. Gaddis (Indic people)
  I. Title
  305.8'9149   DS432.G275

ISBN 0 00 217789 7

First published 1987
© Christina Noble 1987

Set in Monophoto Apollo by Ace Filmsetting Ltd, Frome
Made and printed in Great Britain by
T. J. Press Ltd, Cornwall

Contents

Acknowledgements

I should like to thank Peter Phillimore for all I learnt from his thesis and for his generous co-operation; Simon Weightman of the India Department of the London School of Oriental and African Studies, for his encouragement and help; and David Sumsion, whose line drawings appear in this book on pages 8 and 204.

Illustrations

First Impressions
and the Idea of a Year's Journey

I was on my way from Scotland to Delhi in a Morris Minor Traveller when I first saw Gaddi shepherds. Driving east from Pathankot (in the Punjab) on an October morning we crossed into the state of Himachal Pradesh. At the foot of the Himalayas a flock of milk-white goats and sheep were resting in the shade of a *pipal* tree; kids and lambs frolicked in the striped shade. The shepherds were resting, too, drawing slowly on their hookahs. They wore cloaks of homespun white tweed, kilted by a black rope wound round the waist. It seemed as if a biblical illustration had come to life. I got out of the car to take a photograph and saw that one of the shepherds had two kids tucked into the chest pouch of his cloak. The photograph became a favourite and the scene remained one of the most vivid in my memories of the drive.

That was nearly twenty years ago, and it was the first time I had been to Himachal and the mountains of India. Home was in the West Highlands of Scotland so I knew about hill farming and had learned to gather, dip, crog and clip. When I was six I was given a black lamb as a pet. I sold Sooty for a profit, which I kept for a long time hidden in a drawer – showing an early interest in making money from sheep.

Now for the last fifteen years my husband, who is Indian, our two children and I have lived in Himachal, at Manali at the head of Kulu valley, organizing walking holidays. That is how I came to know so many of the tracks across the West Himalayas and, on early route-finding expeditions, how I began to meet the Gaddis. Unlike most villagers or Khampa herb-gatherers or wandering sadhus, the shepherds consistently gave reliable information about the way ahead. How many hours or days will it take? How difficult? Is there a bridge at the moment? Many of the routes over the remote passes are known only to these shepherds. I speak Hindi and was able to enjoy their courteous and forthright answers. It became a pleasurable excitement to come round a corner, or over the brow of a pass, and see a Gaddi camp; identifiable by the black-and-white check blankets (spread to dry or enclosing a pen of young lambs), by the black-and-tan mastiff-type dogs and by their dry-stone igloo shelters. Often we would be given tea, well boiled, with goat's milk in a brass beaker – very hot to drink from.

But one incident made a lasting impact. We had climbed to a 15,000-foot pass and had spent some time sitting on its crest, absorbing the eerie silence, the manifestation of limitless space and the sense of eternity. Suddenly from the glacier just below we heard a faint bleating. There, caught in the opaque green ice, was a lamb. We picked it up, slithered and 'foot-skied' down the glacier, and were struggling on the loose boulders of the moraine when we saw a shepherd coming up the hill. He had reached his camp far below, having crossed the pass much earlier in the day, and found he was one lamb short. By the time he met us he must have reclimbed a good five miles and 2500 feet. He was astonished that anyone but a shepherd would have bothered to rescue the foundling. A day or two later we reached his village. Here he took me up into his house and insisted that his sister become my *dharm-*

behin (adopted sister). She and I performed a simple ceremony: gave each other three nibbles of *ghi* and three of *gur* (raw sugar), placed a *tika* mark on each other's forehead, touched each other's feet and then embraced – to the right and to the left – twice. For years after, though we seldom met, as her village was a ten-day walk away, we occasionally sent each other presents. She would send tins of *ghi* or the mirror medallions, embroidered with buttons and beads, which Gaddi girls hang from the ends of their plaits or pin to their bodices. And I would send packets of tea or coloured cloth for headscarves.

I found a description of the Gaddis written over a hundred years ago. Their clothes were described as they still are today, and it was obvious the author had found them an attractive people:

'The Gaddis are the most remarkable race in the hills. . . . [They] are a very simple and virtuous race, remarkable even among the hill population for their eminent regard for the truth. Crime is almost unknown, the women are chaste and honest. They are frank and merry in their manners and con-stantly meet together singing and dancing in a style peculiar to themselves. They are great tipplers, and at these festive meetings the natural hilarity is considerably enhanced by deep potations. In person they are a comely race. The women frequently are fair and beautiful, their features regular and their expressions also mild and engaging. The Gaddis wear the thread of caste and are much stricter in Hindu customs and observances than most of the inhabitants of the higher ranges of the Himalayas.'[1]

I, too, was attracted by their appearance, by the idea of their migratory livelihood and by the people themselves: I wanted to know more. The only way would be to follow the pattern of their year.

*

I began in spring and ended in winter. To some extent the journey should be envisaged as a migration from the winter grazing to the summer, as flocks spend a long stretch of time at the summer and the winter pastures. But during the journey there and back, they are not on the move all the time. Shepherds do not really view it as a journey between Lahoul in the summer and the plains of the Punjab in the winter; more as an itinerant life with time spent in different localities. Joining them at the beginning of their migration towards the summer pastures, we crossed the Dhaula Dhar range early in May. But we did not reach Lahoul until early in July – a mere hundred miles in two months. Much of those two months was spent in Gadderan. Many of the shepherds had homes and villages there, and spring grazing was plentiful. The less grazing available, the faster the flocks have to move: they might be forced to cover the fifty miles down the road through Kulu in five days.

At a rough estimate the distance of the circular route I describe would be a little over four hundred miles: the last fifty or sixty I travelled by train and bus, the rest I walked. If I had walked every day without stopping anywhere, my journey would represent about thirty-six walking days, an average of a little under ten miles a day. Shepherds and flocks would take nearly double the number of days; rarely do they cover more than five miles in a day. But they do not – and neither did I – tackle the route as a consecutive trek. Where grazing is limited they go as fast as the flocks are able; when grazing is available they camp for days, or weeks.

My companions for most of the journey were Karma and Tchering, who work as guides for us in Manali, with whom I have trekked for many years and whom I know well. We panted up to the high passes, made sacrifices to the local deities and passed long summer days playing rummy in the sun with the shepherds. I have made many friends – Deori village in the Upper Ravi is my Gaddi home, and Sunni Devi and her family special friends. But I cannot claim that I lived like the Gaddis. Sometimes we did camp with the shepherds themselves, and stayed in their village homes: more often we travelled with our tents and enjoyed the luxury of our own food. I would lie cosily in my sleeping bag, zipped into my tent, while on a rainy night the shepherds sat hunched in a cave or their dry-stone igloo.

The journey ought not so much to be calculated in distances and walking days but more in terms of the variation in altitude. The effect of altitude is crucial to the story. Gaddi shepherds are transhumant people. The dictionary definition of transhumance is 'The seasonal movement of livestock to regions of different climate.' If they were to spend summers down on the plains of the Punjab, the sheep and goats would die, if not of heat at temperatures of 110°F, then of starvation. And if they were to attempt to spend winters in Lahoul at 14,000 feet, they would simply be buried under several feet of snow.

The varying altitude dictates the climate and the vegetation – which direct, and also speed up or slow down, the movement of the flocks. The south-facing slopes of the Dhaula Dhar, at Gaddi village's height of about 5000 feet, might be a different continent from the arid hillside in Lahoul, barely a hundred miles away, but 10,000 feet higher and behind the Himalayan rain shadow. For me it meant that the journey was through some of the most dramatic terrain in the world. Winters are spent among scrub jungle at 2000 feet; the Jalsu pass which we crossed with the flocks in May is 11,000 feet; the villages of the Ravi and the Budil valleys lie at 6000–7000 feet; and the Kugti pass, which we crossed at the end of June, is 16,000 feet. If I could add the thousands of feet we climbed and descended when crossing passes to all the ups and downs that were necessary to avoid a cliff face or to cross from one side of a stream to the other, I might be able to calculate the total elevation lost and gained, but it would remain only a statistic. It would convey no idea of the majesty of the Dhaula Dhar towering above Kangra valley. Nor would it convey the thrill, a week later, having climbed through dark cedar and rhododendron forests, of finally standing between the peaks and, as the early-morning mist perceptibly moved, seeing for the first time the summit of Mount Kailash, Lord Shiva's seat. Nor would it give an idea of the stark mountainsides in Lahoul, above the treeline, mercilessly eroded by a dry wind and frost, where vegetation can only thrive when watered by snow-melt – where gentians and blue poppies grow among glacial rubble.

My quest was to find out about the lives of the shepherds. It would have been a pointless venture if I had not been able to see them against the background of these mountains. The landscape is without scale. The human eye cannot measure it, nor words nor the camera's lens illustrate its grandeur. Its most arresting aspect is the insignificance of man's efforts; by the side of the mountains they appear trifling and insubstantial. Yet when you look closer you are mesmerised by the intricate pattern of the terraces contouring down the valley. They are the results of centuries of labour; these tiny strips grow the wheat, barley, rice, pulses and potatoes on which most of Himachal's people depend for their subsistence. Then, at the head of a valley, you might spot a cluster of white dots: a flock barely discernible among the rocks and maggot-like in proportion to the surrounding landscape. To you their track is hardly visible, but the shepherds and flocks may have followed it for generations. And by the end of my journey I was to realise that the flock of white dots was not insignificant; it was worth some ten thousand pounds.

1. *Punjab District Gazetteer 1906*, Kangra District Part A, from the *Settlement Report* by J. B. Lyall.

CHAPTER ONE

Up and Over the Dhaula Dhar

The spring migration from Kangra to Gadderan

The early-morning bus from Baijnath shuddered and roared up the 1000 feet and 10 miles to the road-end at the Binwa hydro-electric project. Binwa (4500 feet) is at the foot of the Jalsu pass (11,200 feet), the lowest of the passes across the Dhaula Dhar range and therefore the first to open and the last to close. The bus was jammed; the passengers included a sheep and two goats and their three kids. A miscellany of baggage was piled on the roof – blanket bundles, tin trunks, baskets, plastic jerry cans and buckets, drums, rush mats and cooking pans – I assumed it was all to be carried over the pass: the Gaddis were returning home for the summer.

It was May. Down on the plains of the Punjab the temperature would be well over 100° and the air thick with dust blown about by a hot wind. Birds, animals and those who lead a migratory life moved towards the cool of the hills. North from the plains the first Himalayan range, the Sivaliks, at their highest a mere 4000 feet, bring little relief. But once into Kangra valley the sight of the Dhaula Dhar delights the enervated spirit with the prospect of cooler air. 'Dhaula Dhar' means 'the white range', and a pilgrim approaching it for the first time might well believe the shining white peaks were the world's highest. For the great thrust of mountains rises straight up 12,000–14,000 feet from the valley floor.

In the spring the weather, too, moves up from the south. In the afternoons magnificent thunder clouds begin to roll across Kangra valley; the rising heat from the plains clashes with the cold air from the evaporating snow. With surprising speed the clouds gather and darken the sky. Even the leaves on the trees become dark. Then shafts of white light slash through the blackness, so searing that you blink. The dramatic forked lightning that represents the disturbed mood of lovers in the old Kangra pictures is no exaggeration. Resounding roars of thunder follow. Sometimes a cloud bursts and sheds itself; though the rain may be falling half a mile away, you can smell the sweet-sour smell of water soaking the hot earth. By late evening the storm is spent. The remaining clouds gather and disappear, leaving the towering Dhaula Dhar an unearthly purple colour. It looks more like a flat theatre backdrop than a three-dimensional range of forest, waterfall, granite and snow.

But now, in the early morning, every detail was clear. The jacaranda trees were at their best; the blossom a soft, intense blue that somehow does not clash with the sky. The contours of the terracing were as clearly defined as an etching. And in the distance small ridges and knolls were topped with a silhouette of *chil* pine, like a fringe of hair standing on end.

Past a few stands of pine, the bus lurched round the corner and, as though all its energy was spent, stopped among the desecration of the Binwa hydel project. Karma, Tchering and I stood stunned in the middle of the squalor – corrugated iron, twisted pipes and crumbling concrete. My romantic idea of joining the Gaddis' spring migration was shattered. By the time we had managed to gather our wits and had bought rope to tie our kit bags and tents to the carrying frames, everyone from the bus and all their baggage had vanished. Where to? Tchering had been over the Jalsu once when he was fifteen – that was ten years ago – long before work on the project began. Where was the path out of this mess? Then a young Gaddini (female Gaddi) wearing a new dress, an elegant turquoise chiffon scarf and bangles up to her elbow came out of a tea shop and shouldered a check blanket-bundle, tightening its goat-hair ropes over her velvet bodice. She was followed by a middle-aged man. Yes, they were heading over the Jalsu pass into the Ravi valley, in Gadderan. They would show us the way.

The Gaddini was plump and, encumbered by her baggage and her long full skirt, found the steep climb and the hot sun as trying as I did. We struggled up a perpendicular gravel slope between the hovels of the Nepali labourers, numbed by the roar of a pneumatic drill; and 1500 feet up, at the first shade (a mutilated oak tree), we found the one sheep and two goat owners, our co-passengers from the bus. One of the little girls had left her newly bought plastic shoes at Binwa and had been sent back down in the vain hope of finding them.

Our companion-guides turned out to be father (a widower) and daughter. He had married off his two elder daughters and, though our friend was already twenty, he was not in a hurry to make arrangements for her betrothal as he was loath to part with her. His son, he explained with pride, was a clerk in a fertiliser plant in Meerut, far away in Uttar Pradesh. Father and daughter had spent the winter with relations in Kangra and now were on their way home to Bajoli, a village in the upper Ravi valley. We looked forward to each other's company for the next four or five days, at least until we were in Gadderan proper.

At last we reached longed-for shade: a rhododendron

forest.[1] Some of the trees stood forty feet high, their scarlet flowers already withered. But there was still no drinking water. So it was a great relief when we rounded a corner and the father pointed to some flat ground ahead, crowded with sheep, goats and people: here there was water. It was a popular resting place, a sociable scene. There must have been six or seven flocks; had you been looking down from the cliffs above, you might have thought the place was strewn with off-white, rounded rocks, grouped in six or seven irregular circles. Shepherds and their families, encircled by their flocks, rested on the ground; lying back against their packs or sitting cross-legged round a fire, cooking. Under a projecting rock there was a Gaddi-owned tea hotel; locally made liquor was also available. The hotelier was engaged in untying a dead sheep from a mule's saddle. It had been killed by a falling stone up ahead, and the shepherd had persuaded a passing muleteer, returning from delivering rations over the pass, to carry it here. Our guides disappeared to join relations, with a flock, who were already cooking.

We sank down in the cool, damp shade of the cave-like hotel and drank a welcome glass of tea. The hotelier provided us with a ladleful of live coals to start our fire and with a little persuasion sold us the sheep's liver. So within half an hour we had a feast of chapattis and half-fried liver. Over the years Karma, Tchering and I have often walked together through the hills and know each other's habits and tastes. Both of them are Buddhists, to whom the idea of butchering is anathema. I have known Tchering, the younger, to slaughter a sheep when there was no one else who would: I have never seen Karma do it. But, like most Himalayan Buddhists, they relish meat-eating. Replete, we lay back against our haversacks in the shade and slept.

Around three o'clock we prepared to move on. Our guide came over to explain that he very much wanted to go with us, but that his in-laws, who had decided to spend the night here, had insisted on their staying, and his daughter was tired. He was sure we would meet tomorrow.

The valley we climbed up was green and lush. The sun only intermittently penetrated the white oak and rhododendron forest, and creepers and thick undergrowth demonstrated the high rainfall on this, the southern side of the Dhaula Dhar. We spent an hour or more enraptured, watching langur monkeys on the far bank of the river. There must have been four or five hundred of them. Grandfathers stood sentinel on prominent rocks while youngsters practised swinging on the creepers and hurling themselves from tree to tree. Their white faces and black noses and eyes are surprisingly well camouflaged, and it was a minute or two before we spotted a mother gobbling some succulent shoots; a baby, hardly bigger than a human hand, clasped tightly to her chest.

Without our guides we had no difficulty in finding our way. The footpath up the Parai *nala* (*nala* meaning a valley or river) is the main route from Kangra over into Gadderan, though it is only a slippery, stony path, barely a track. But even those not driving flocks prefer it to the long way round via Pathankot and Chamba, by bus and jeep. The path delves under oak and rhododendron trees, skirts huge bamboos, and burrows between box and laurel scrub. The goats greedily reached up on their hind legs to crane for juicy shoots and the kids climbed up into the trees. The sheep were less happy; the undergrowth was too dense for grass.

We had been walking for two days before we met our original guides again. At 5.30 in the morning, as we were packing before climbing to the pass, the father appeared on the skyline. His jolly daughter came puffing and panting up the hill, hitching up her skirts; she had been joined by a group of friends. By this time we had become accustomed to the journey and had begun to feel part of a pilgrimage. The travellers chattered and asked questions as they walked, when they stopped to smoke *biris* on a shaded rock, or settled to cook and eat. I much enjoyed each day's walk, making new acquaintances or meeting old friends again. It was as intriguing as being among passengers on board ship, but less claustrophobic. Jokes and incidents that happened on the way were retold and embellished for the benefit of those who had missed them. A long-haired young man wearing jeans, who claimed to be a sadhu, was mercilessly teased for his incapacity to climb the hill, and for failing to hold his liquor. The jokes and the camaraderie had a *Canterbury Tales* atmosphere. An old woman told me so many incidents from her life – the splendours of her marriage, then the tragedy of two children dying in infancy, and the lack of sons to till the fields – that I began to feel I had known her for years.

I had soon realized that on the spring migration, north from Kangra to Gadderan, it is not only shepherds and flocks who are on the move. From late April into June men, women and children straggle over the passes. Sitting in the shade of a yew, smoking a *biri*, I asked our guide why it was that whole households seemed to be on the move. Why had they not spent the winter at their home villages in Gadderan?

'Well, it's cold there, and snowy, there's not much to eat, crops aren't good there. Anyway Gaddi people always move south for the winter, just like Lord Shiva moves from Gadderan and his summer seat on Mount Kailash down to Pujalpur for the winter.'

'But,' I said, 'in Kulu where the highest villages are at about the same height, six to seven thousand feet, and even in Lahoul where the villages are much higher, only a few people go away in the winter.'

'You see,' he explained, 'we are a shepherding people. We are in the habit of going with the flocks: it is because of the *dharma* that Lord Shiva gave us. It happened like this. The gods were making their way through the Himalayas. They came to a particularly high, snow-covered pass. They struggled and struggled to get over it but failed. In despair they sat down, tired and bad-tempered. Lord Shiva was the angriest. [He often gave vent to terrible bouts of rage.] In a fury he took a pinch of dirt from his body and hurled it to the ground – out of his dirt sheep and goats were created. The flock walked across the snow and as they went they made a path. Then, following that path, the gods were able to cross the pass. In thanks Shivji [the familiar name for Lord Shiva] gave the Gaddis the privilege of looking after the flocks. But these days it is very difficult, so young men, like my son, are going into the army, government service and shopkeeping. That's good, but it's not our *dharma*.'

There were men and women who looked old enough to have crossed this way twice a year for three score years and ten, and there were babies of a few weeks. Babies and young children were carried sideways, across the rest of the luggage, on the mother's or father's back. They were often not tethered into a shawl – the usual way in the hills – but perched, the parent casually holding on to a leg or a foot while the child's head dangled down the other side. And all the purchases made during the winter were being taken home – hens proudly carried in the crook of an arm, handsome spotted house goats with large udders, Jersey-type heifers and young bulls, baskets, winnowing trays, plastic water-cans, brightly coloured nylon sweaters, radios and drums. It was not only the families of those who had flocks who were on their way home. Some people had spent the winter working as servants, rice-huskers, road workers or agricultural labourers. Others had been spinning and weaving. Some owned property in Kangra as well as in Gadderan. Now it would take them a week or more to get back to their home villages.

Not everyone walked exactly the same stage every day.

Those with flocks and the old and lame covered a shorter distance. Our day started early. Up before dawn and off soon after, walking (with plenty of rests for a smoke and a chat) until eleven or twelve o'clock when we all stopped to eat (some settled down to cook; others brought a picnic of chapattis and vegetables) and to snooze. We and some of the others would then walk another three or four hours before settling for the night's camp. At places there were rough stone huts; in Scotland they would be called 'sheilings'. More often, travellers sheltered in caves or under projecting rocks; the first to arrive taking possession of the most comfortable. In these hills you do not find reasonable camping grounds wherever you might want them: flat ground is rare, and a camp must have wood and water nearby. All the sites at appropriate stages along the way were busy. No one except us had their own tents, and as we pitched them they immediately aroused interest. Old men would gently stroke the cloth and shepherds would admire how lightweight the sleeping bags were; everyone wanted to know the cost of our equipment, and our boots were particularly admired.

Firewood was only a problem at the highest camp, so normally all hearths were burning soon after arrival. Everyone had their own cooking pots, girdles for chapattis and water-cans. We, like others, picked the young nettles that grow so prolifically round camping grounds and so had green vegetables with our rice and dal. Our provisions were similar to the shepherds' except that I had brought a jar of Marmite and some eggs for treats, and we had a supply of dried milk. By dusk food had been cooked and eaten, and cooking pots washed – theirs were much better burnished than ours. They spread blankets on the ground and covered themselves with more blankets – black-and-white bundles in circles round the dying embers – while we zipped ourselves into our tents.

One night at the far end of the camping ground there was a

'hotel'-cum-liquor-stall. Soon after I had zipped up my tent I heard drunken ribaldry and oaths, unmistakably the long-haired sadhu. I envisaged his staggering into my tent and I knew that my screams for help would be drowned by the roar of the fast-flowing stream nearby. I grabbed my sleeping bag and ran across to the protection of a rather startled Karma and Tchering.

Himachali women are not given to veiling their faces, nor are they constrained by purdah, but the Gaddinis were particularly outgoing; not just towards me but to everyone they met along the way – men, too. So much so that I was surprised to see a girl quickly pull her headcloth over her face when a shepherd unexpectedly came out of a tea shop: it turned out that he was an in-law, and in the presence of a male in-law modesty requires it. Gaddinis' headcloths are large cotton squares, worn more like a shawl than a scarf, decorated with embroidered – often hand-embroidered – flowers. Their long, very full dresses, called *luancharis*, reminded me of the gathered, swirling skirts in *pahari* woodcarvings and in the old Kangra and Chamba paintings. The long-sleeved bodice is made of velvet, with bands of contrasting colours round the wrists and the V neck. It is attached, just above the waist, to the skirt. The latter requires 12 metres of floral cotton or hand-printed coarse chintz – the hem may measure 44 feet and is 'trimmed' with four bands of contrasting colours. The whole garment, complete with all trimmings and linings, needs eight different pieces of cloth. A few women wore *luancharis* of undyed white tweed – like the shepherds' cloaks but down to the ground – and the lapels were stitched with embroidered rosettes. The *luanchari* is bound at the waist with a *dora* – a rope wound round and round. The full skirt of the *luanchari* must be warm, but also terribly heavy and cumbersome. No wonder when they were struggling uphill they often hitched the front round to the back, tucked into the *dora*. But the Gaddinis do not like to be seen out and about without their long skirts: only at home, or when camp is reached, do they strip down to the Punjabi-style pyjama and overshirt which they wear underneath.

In rural India savings are seldom entrusted to a bank; they are sometimes kept as gold coins hidden in house walls or under the floor, more often they are treasured as jewellery. The safest way to protect your wealth, particularly if you are in the habit of being on the move, is to wear it. The Gaddinis were walking savings accounts. Some had more than others but no one was without bangles, one or two necklaces and earrings. They had large gold earrings, heavy, flat, gold discs pinned into the nostril, hair ornaments, silver and gold necklaces with amber or colourful enamel pendants – many depicting Lord Shiva and his consort Parvati. And all wore simple silver pendants embossed with crude representations of their ancestors.

Gaddinis even decorate their skin – their chins were patterned with delicate circles of tattooed dots, and geometrical designs were tattooed on to the backs of their hands and lower arms. All wear distinctively Gaddi medallions – mirrors encircled with beads and buttons – which girls and women stitch and give to each other, to friends and relations, and also to their menfolk, as tokens of affection. Women wear them hanging from the waist, pinned on lapels or attached to the end of their plait along with their bunch of keys.

Every woman I met asked me the same question: 'Where are your children?' Throughout India unmarried and barren women are considered pitiable, but the Gaddis even feel it necessary to erect stones to quieten the spirits of childless couples; otherwise their unhappy spirits will wander at night, and disturb everyone's sleep with their wailing. I was relieved to be able to answer that my two children were safely at home in Manali.

It is hard to describe fully the all-pervasive sheep-and-goatiness of that journey. Whenever I glanced at a distant hillside, vaguely admiring the skyline or the precipitous rock face, I would realize it was 'lifting' with milk-white flocks. They were clustered in an irregular circle round a midday camp, moving imperceptibly across the hillside grazing, or following each other in single file along an invisible path, like maggots. If you were near to them, there was endless baa-ing and bleating and calling, grunting and whistling. The whistling was not, as you might have imagined, at the dogs, but at the goats and sheep. A shepherd leads the flock, calling and whistling; another comes behind, urging on the stragglers. Along the way the stink of wool and dung was overwhelming. The sharp little hoofs ate away the track and the dung made the rocks slippery. They walked slower than we did, but when we were caught among them on a narrow path their irregular pace was maddening: they would suddenly run on, and those we had with difficulty pushed our way past were ahead again.

Our last camp below the pass was up above the lush forest. The colours and light here were peculiar. The brown oak, *Quercus semicarpifolia*, has such dark green leaves that, in contrast to their orange undersides, they look slaty grey, almost black. And the undersides of the leaves of the *Rhododendron campanulatum* are also orange, its branches silvery. In the woods the ground was still streaked with glistening snow, and with the slanting light of the setting sun the colours were almost supernatural.

Here we camped beside a large family. The grandfather was ill. Two grown-up sons came to our fireside to ask for medicine. They had sold their flocks last year as they had needed the cash (I thought it would be too nosy to ask why). The grandmother and her daughter, Shanti, who was the mother of five young children, wore beautiful undyed *luancharis*. Shanti came over to lend us a brass vessel to fetch water and settled

25

down by our fire to suckle her youngest child and to talk, while knitting a sweater for an older child. She said her husband and his flock were in Gharwal (Uttar Pradesh). Because he could only get grazing rights to pasture so far away, winter and summer, she never saw him. (This would seem to question the paternity of her five children, but I did not like to ask about that, either.) She was travelling with her brothers on her way home to her in-laws in the Upper Ravi. She told me she was Khatri caste and asked what I was. It was too confusing to try to explain why Europeans do not have a caste, so I claimed my husband's. And neither Karma nor Tchering, both Buddhists, owned up to being casteless; both claimed Rajput status. So, insidiously, Hindu caste-consciousness grows on everyone.

Our conversation was interrupted by the roar of an ill-tuned radio: out of the darkness emerged a tall figure wrapped in a check blanket – a shepherd from the camp above. He, too, gathered himself into the circle squatting at our fireside, and turned down Radio Simla, just a little. His winter grazing – he had a flock of 350 – was down near Bilaspur. The family had property near Baijnath and at Nayagraon in the Upper Ravi. But he complained, 'It is very bad work, day after day going with the flock. Sometimes it's too hot, sometimes it's too cold. Then you have to take the sheep and goats up dangerous places where there are wild animals and falling stones. And what do you get in return? A chapatti or two in the evening. That's all.'

It was about eight o'clock on a clear morning when we reached the summit of the Jalsu pass. I had climbed the last, steep stretch (it was slippery snow) with my new friend, Shanti, mother of the five children, giving a hand to her six-year-old – even he had a bundle roped to his back. We passed a young billy goat being pulled up the path by the scruff of its neck. It had eaten *kashmiri patta* (*Rhododendron campanulatum*).

Though it is very poisonous, the hungry sheep and goats occasionally feed on it when fodder is scarce: it makes them *nasha* (drunk). If several of the flock are suffering, it is difficult for the shepherd to keep them all on the move, and he hurls stones and swears at the unfortunate animals.

At the top we sat in the snow. As we watched, the early-morning mist lifted and we gazed at the pure white beauty of Mount Kailash, 19,000 feet, Lord Shiva's seat. I had often heard of it but never seen it before. I could see why it has been incorporated into local mythology and is revered as the heart, or soul, of Gadderan. It stands alone, an elongated pyramid. At the cairn-like shrine on top of the pass we all offered flowers, primulas, irises and anemones. Our companions were relieved to see the hills of home again. Shanti's brothers begged me to photograph them and their largest billy goat with Mount Kailash in the distance: obviously they thought it an appropriate background for a formal photograph.

Then with cries of delight we slithered down a very steep snow slide. One thousand five hundred feet below it was clear of snow again and we settled on the gentian- and primula-dotted turf to rest and eat. Chapattis, both wheat and maize, were shared and exchanged, and fried nettles or bracken. The drunk goat let out a terrible groan and vomited. We snoozed for a while, waiting for the ill grandfather. Our group was scattered among stony mounds: Gujars' graves, I was told. Gujars are buffalo herdsmen, Muslims: they have permanent summer grazing up here. Shanti told me that many were murdered here at the time of the partition troubles in 1947. It seemed so improbable that religious mass murders could happen here on this remote, peaceful alp. Their substantial, flat-roofed, single-storeyed houses, belonging to the survivors' descendants, were still empty; they would arrive for the summer in a month or so.

The Gujars' houses were not the only sign of summer

visitors. Just above where we were sitting there was a dwelling carefully built into a protecting rock. It, too, was empty at the moment, but Tchering explained that on his previous trip over the Jalsu he had come here. It was his uncle's place: a hotel, a liquor *batti* and, most important, the headquarters of his *tejbuta* enterprise. *Tejbuta* is a valuable wild root, harvested for processing into incense and as Ayurvedic medicine. His uncle has bought the licence to collect it in this area and employs forty Nepali labourers here throughout the summer.

Stretched on the turf in the warm midday sun I wondered at the fortitude and enterprise of shepherds, buffalo herdsmen and traders who wrest a living out of these massive and, one would have imagined, empty mountains.

At last the old man arrived, tired and dejected. He had been caught up by a prosperous-looking couple: the woman was fat, which is unusual in the hills, and boasted a quantity of heavy jewellery. They were travelling with five pretty girls, and their cows, goats and many newly purchased household goods. We prepared to move on, and those who had put on goat-hair socks for extra grip on the snow tucked them into their packs. And we were off, tripping through the rhododendrons, sniffing the air of home with happy anticipation.

Later that day we overtook a sad couple with a goat. The man was so weak he could move only when supported by his wife. The goat, too, was sick; perhaps 'drunk' from *kashmiri patta*, but I felt it was a more permanent illness. The old woman had tears in her eyes: everyone had gone on and left them alone. She would help her husband as far as a supportive rock or tree and leave him there while she went back to fetch the goat. It was hard to imagine how the three of them had negotiated the pass, and, if they did reach home, that they would ever set off on another migration.

That night was particularly noisy. A series of little fires

along the hillside showed how many families were camped in caves or tucked under overhanging rocks. Shanti walked up and down in a hopeless attempt to soothe and quieten her howling baby. After the day's exertions she had no milk for it. For the same reason neither did the ewes or nanny goats. So there was no goat's milk available to give the baby and none for the lambs or kids. Karma mixed some dried milk. Shanti put the glass, hot, to the baby's lips; she laughed when it howled even louder than before. So she drank it herself (I was a little shocked at her callousness).[2] I could not sleep until some time in the early hours of the morning, when the ravenous baby and the kids and lambs must have been exhausted and the pitiful crying and bleating ceased.

Before we reached the Ravi river, I and many others – men, women and children – were coming down a 1000-foot drop to cross a side-stream. On the far side the path zig-zagged up an equally steep slope. Halfway up it a shepherd began to take his flock off the track. The flock scattered across the precipitous hillside to graze. One of our companions bellowed across the gorge, ordering the shepherd not to do so, as dislodged stones would fall on the people climbing up. The shepherd paid no heed. We settled on a rock on the near side, to wait until the flock moved on and the danger of falling stones was over. As we watched, a fully grown sheep came hurtling down through the air, legs outstretched, and fell with a deathly thud on the path. We gasped: there was silence for a while, and then everyone noisily vented their disapproval of the shepherd. And, when we crossed by a rickety bridge (a new Public Works Department one having been washed away), we saw a freshly dead cow with a broken neck in the river bed.

At the top of the hill above the gorge, there was a temple to Lakhna Devi (a form of Parvati), the presiding deity of the area, whose power had been so dramatically illustrated. One of the shepherds of the ill-mannered (and ill-fated) flock was sitting by the temple. He was roundly abused. 'What do you think you were doing, taking flocks across a hill like that in the middle of the day, with mothers and children walking up the path below? What sort of Gaddi do you think you are! See, you have no respect for the *Devi*.' And we were told the story of how the cow had died. Her owner, nearing the end of a five-day journey from Kangra, had got drunk and while she was negotiating the steep slope he had hit her in a fit of temper. She had lost her balance and fallen to her death. The story was told us to emphasize the fate of those, like the shepherd, who show a wanton lack of respect for the *Devi*. The general reaction was that she was justified in asserting her power.

As we descended towards the Ravi valley, our companions gradually began to turn off on to even smaller paths leading up the hill or across the river towards their villages. The fraternity of the pilgrimage spirit began to loosen as the excitement of nearing home increased. 'Kangra is better than here in the winter, but there you never feel hungry. It's the water [we would say "It's the air"]. Here you enjoy your food.'

In Gadderan the mountains go straight down into the river gorges. Down at the bottom there were no signs of villages or cultivation, there was only the infernal noise of the river; in fact it was difficult to imagine that there were villages above. But at 1000 feet above the floor of the valley, there are views on a scale that defy one's usual visual experience. Shiny snow peaks are clearly chiselled in the evening sun, and become ethereal in the moonlight. Waterfalls cascade in white sprays down the rock faces. There are dark forests of deodar, spruce and fir, particularly on the north-facing slopes. On the south-facing slopes, sometimes even very high up, are stripes of deep green or yellow. These are tiny cultivated terraces, some of them so narrow that the terracing has to be open-ended to allow bullocks pulling a plough to turn, while others have to

30

be dug by hand, where the slope is too precipitous for bullocks.

The villages and their setting are extraordinarily pretty. The houses are substantially, and skilfully, built of massive timbers (no nails: wooden pegs) and dry stone. Some have living quarters on the ground floor, though more often these are byres for cattle and the usual living quarters are on the first floor. Projecting wooden verandas run the length of the building – arched and decorated with carvings of birds and animals. The roofs are made of lengths of vertical timber. Every house, or group of two or three houses, has a paved courtyard. Some houses were still shut up for the winter and were a little ghostly – as though the owners might have gone for ever. The heavy wooden doors were padlocked, the locks dusty from disuse, and shrines in the courtyards unattended. As all the cattle had been left in the charge of the few families who remained for the winter, most of the byre doors had been protected against weather and intruders by being plastered over with mud and dung. I noticed that in places it had crumbled at the corners, gnawed by hungry rats trying to get in. The only signs of life were the bees flying into hives made of hollowed sections of timber set into the walls of the houses. Heaps of manure, accumulated the previous year and matured during the winter, lay in the yards or on the paths, waiting to be carried out to the fields.

At Nayagraon village some of the returning families had already reached home. Bedding 'quilts', made of bits of old tweed blankets roughly quilted, had been spread in the sun to air. But there was no hustle or bustle, no sweeping or cleaning. A family we had met on the way had arrived home just ahead of us. They were sitting on the stone balustrade of their front yard, passing round a hookah, and gossiping. They waved to us to come and join them. Several people came to call – the younger one casually touched the feet of anyone older in greeting and then joined the line sitting on the balustrade, to hear and to give news. It all happened slowly – there were no excited outpourings. Conversation had a West Highland pace.

Out of the twenty-five or thirty houses in the village there were half a dozen which were newly built, and more under construction (in the traditional style). Here, most of the households owned flocks and the people were obviously prosperous. There was a shop in the village which stocked a surprising variety of goods. There were several different qualities of rice, varieties of dal in wooden chests, and shelves stacked with tins of dried milk, soap, matches, *biris*, manufactured cooking fat, bolts of cloth, tea-strainers, hand-carders and shoes. A young man shouldered a sack of rice: the sack was a goatskin and, re-inflated with rice, it was almost lifelike, its four legs sticking out behind, its neck used as the neck of the sack.

The shop was also a social centre. Women sat on the wooden benches inside and the men sat outside, enjoying a glass of tea and a smoke. The young man rested his goatskin pack on the bench while he stopped to talk to us. He said he was a Brahmin from a village high above (near the temple to the powerful Lakhna Devi). His ambition was to become the postmaster. He spoke of the deity with awe and explained that she is a form of Parvati (Shiva's consort). He wanted us to appreciate how powerful she is. . . .

'You know how big Jawalamurkhi town is in Kangra, because so many people go there to receive her *darshan* [sight or experience]? Well, if a *devi* who had power like Lakhna Devi was in Kangra a whole city would have to be built, so many pilgrims would want to come for her blessing. But here hardly anyone comes from the outside; it is very quiet. At the time of the pilgrimage to Manimahesh lake (at the foot of Mount Kailash) they come, but not here to Bramour and up the Budil valley. Here it is very wild country.'

32

opposite: Flocks on the lowest hairpin bend climb towards Lakhna temple.

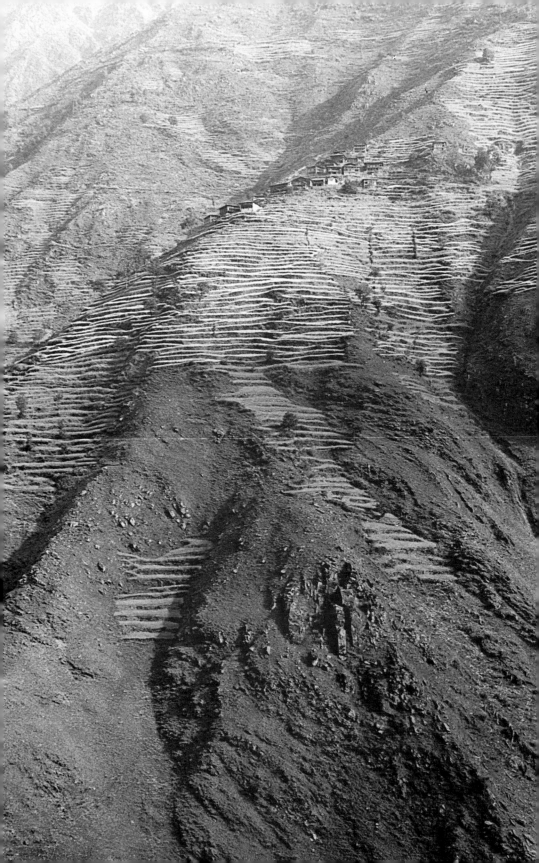

left: Village and terracing on the steep slopes of the Upper Ravi valley.

right: The verandah of Sunni Devi's house in Deori (Sunni Devi on the right).

A Gaddini prepares to tie her *dora*

A child, in his homespun jacket and cap, standing outside the Lakhna shrine above Nayagraon.

below: Two Gaddinis pose for a photograph, wearing their head ornaments, which are reserved for special occasions, and *chiri* (medallions).

above: Pal Singh and his brother, the *pradhan*, smoking hookahs on the verandah.

right: A Gaddini carrying her pack and child – the latter perched in the Gaddi style across her back.

below: Flocks resting in the *Chaurasi,* Bramour.

right: Manimahesh Lake (13,000 feet), with Mount Kailash as a backdrop. A devotee stands at the edge of the water, preparing to immerse himself.

overleaf: The Budil valley. A horizontal path stretches across mid-hill and there is a terracing to be seen in the gully above.

He shouldered his pack and set off up the hill, through the forests. In a back courtyard two men were skinning a sheep, which had been killed that morning by a black bear in the forest not far above the village.

We had been travelling for five days. That night we reached the main Ravi valley and camped near the fat, bejewelled woman and her five girls (all dressed in fashionable velvet-bodiced *luancharis*). No wonder she was so fat and so raucously domineering: her husband, the leader of the entourage, was a man of some substance, a Brahmin and the *sarpanch* (head-man) of a large village. He was well educated, very much a gentleman, and spoke courteously and with assurance.

'No, we don't marry our daughters to anyone who isn't a Brahmin, nor our sons, either. You see, people refer to us as being Gaddis because we come from Gadderan, but we aren't really. The Gaddi castes are Rajput and Khatri. We consider ourselves Bramouri Brahmins because we come from Bramour [the headquarters of Gadderan]. Normally we marry Bramouri Brahmins, though nowadays those of us who have property in Kangra do give our daughters to Kangra Brahmins. But though they [Kangra Brahmins] know we are good families and don't lack anything, they don't marry their daughters to our sons so much. They don't like the idea of coming over here to such a faraway place. Yes, yes, we Brahmins own flocks, too, like the Gaddis do; I have a flock of three hundred and my wife's brothers have six hundred.' His message was clear: he wanted me to understand that they considered themselves a cut above most of our travelling companions.

I watched his daughters and nieces spend an hour and a half on the niceties of cleanliness. Down by the spring they chatted and, sitting back on their heels, giggled as they meticulously washed a stack of brass vessels with ash. Then

41

opposite: The Budil valley. A horizontal path stretches across mid-hill and there is terracing to be seen in the gully above.

they scrubbed their hands and faces and finally spent ten minutes rubbing charcoal into their teeth and gums. Dishwashing was not boys' work: the only brother, a twelve-year-old, sat watching from the bank above, fondling a goat and singing.

The next day we hoped to reach Deori village, where we had promised to visit a shepherding family. The walk down the valley was a delight: jasmine, delphiniums and irises were in bloom on the edges of the terraces, the river was an opaque aquamarine, and alders shaded the valley floor. We passed mule trains on their way up carrying grain, *gur* and salt – ordinary rock salt and the black salt that is so necessary to the flocks. Fields were green with winter wheat and barley, while on the fallow terraces men shouted and grunted at their bullocks as they prepared the ground for maize.

After the long and hot day's walk we were daunted by the prospect of climbing up to Deori. Karma and Tchering said they had had enough; it was too hot and too steep – we could see the village 1500 feet up a perpendicular hillside. We sat beside the path in some inadequate shade and slept. By 3.30 p.m. the shadows were lengthening and I persuaded them to struggle on up. Five boys, on their way back from school in Holi, the headquarters of the upper Ravi, kept us company on the endless zig-zags, until they could bear our slow pace no longer and scampered up to wait at a stone bench outside a temple. There they poked their hands down into the rocks to find the (very unripe) apricots they had hidden on their way to school in the morning. At that moment an older brother came along the hill with his flock. He was arriving at his village after the winter, after seven months away from home. All he said was 'Hey, Chandu, take my luggage home!' – and he dropped his blanket-wrapped pack on the path for the youngster to pick up.

There was no flurry of excitement to welcome returning

shepherds and their flocks; no outward signs of emotion. Later that evening the shepherd we had seen on the way up came along the path. He saw his sister-in-law was on the balustrade; he took a red handkerchief from his pocket and covered his head before greeting her; he touched her feet, embraced her, twice on each side, and went on his way.

We camped under a mulberry tree beside a courtyard. Three hundred sheep and goats were penned there for the night. We had been feasted on *rajma* dal, mint chutney and maize chapattis. Exhausted and content, I lay in my tent looking out at the Dhaula Dhar framed by mulberry branches. In the moonlight the snow peaks were almost pale green, and they seemed suspended above the dark forest. There were a few twinkling lights from the villages below, and I could just see the shadows of the terracing. Then nearby, from within the village, came the sound of men and women singing in answering verses. I wanted to get up to go and join the romantic scene; I assumed it must be a welcome for the return-ing shepherds. But I was too comfortable and sleepy to move.

In the morning I was disillusioned: the singing had been Radio Simla – the schoolteacher had loudspeakers in his garden.

1. *Rhododendron arboreum.*

2. Someone to whom I told this story suggested the mother's behaviour would be explained if the baby had been a girl – as on the plains only male children are indulged and cherished. I do not remember if it was a boy or a girl, but nothing I have seen of the Gaddis' attitude to their children suggests a lack of concern towards their daughters – and until recently (in some cases continuing today) it was the groom's family who paid the dowry price.

CHAPTER TWO

Deori, My Village Home

Late spring

In late spring (the end of May to early June) on their way to the high summer pastures, and in early autumn (the middle to the end of September) on their way back down, shepherds and flocks spend a couple of weeks in the vicinity of their home villages. I was made so welcome at Deori and so enjoyed being there that I, too, spent time there.

Sunni Devi and I met on my first morning in Deori down at the spring, where, soon after dawn, the women come to fill their water-pots. They were helping each other lift the heavy, brimful pots on to their heads; resting each one on a thick circle of twisted hay to keep it steady. Then they moved off down the path, their full-skirted *luancharis* swinging. I had been sitting watching. As she passed, Sunni Devi stopped to talk to me and then asked me back to her house.

Her kitchen-living room was large. The only light was through the door from the veranda and through a very small window above the *chulha* (hearth). Coming into the room from the veranda, in from the bright sun, it took a while before my eyes became sufficiently accustomed to the lack of light to see anything. In the initial darkness the first objects

that emerged were some white spots and small circles of re-
flecting mirror. After a while I realized they were decorations
on the old chests that stood against the walls; the timber was
darkened with age. The chests are made with wooden pegs
instead of nails, and the pegs jut out at each end. The dal,
maize and wheat grown in the fields are stored in them, and
also the rice, sugar and tea which have to be brought in from
outside. They are used for storing clothes and blankets, too,
and, hidden away in a secret corner, there may be a treasure
like a box of matches or a poke of white sugary sweets. The
chulha was in the far corner; the window above looked out
over the massive timber doorway, the entrance from the
village path into her courtyard. The window also acted as a
chimney and its sill was a larder for spices and small bottles
of oil. The spotlessly clean floor was plastered with a mixture
of mud and cow dung. It was slightly textured with finger-
marks – I could see how the plasterer had moved across the
floor, smoothing out the surface with her hands. Above the
chests hung balls of spun wool, grey-brown from the smoke,
and there was more in a basket, much whiter because it had
been spun more recently. There was a spinning wheel in the
corner; not like a Western one, more like the *chakra* that
Mahatma Gandhi encouraged every household to use. A lot
of wool is still spun, by both men and women, without a
wheel, by hand on a drop spindle. It is useful as it can be
carried about in a pocket and people can spin on their way to
work in the fields, or sitting chatting on the balustrade.
Weaving is often men's work; the loom was out on the
veranda on a special platform built into the side of the house.

The ceiling was of timber and, like the chests, black with
age and smoke. Set into it, above the *chulha*, there were two
elegant brackets; I could not imagine what they were for until
it was explained that they supported a reinforcement for the
chulha in the room above.

Sunni Devi's sister-in-law lives above. 'They are very troublesome people,' she whispered as she plaited her younger daughter's hair. She was busy getting her ready for school, making sure she had eaten, was properly washed and neatly dressed. Though Gaddi schoolchildren are entitled to a Scheduled Caste and Tribe subsidy, books, slates, pens and ink, and particularly school-going clothes, are a considerable expenditure for the family. For, although it is all right for children to run around the village in any old rags and barefoot, it would be an embarrassment to send them to school without a neat chemise and pyjama, or shirt and shorts. The eldest daughter, Munni, does not go to school as she is needed to take the cows out to graze and to look after her brother, the two-year-old Soban, while Sunni Devi works in the fields.

A man came in, who I assumed must be her husband. He did acknowledge my presence with a passing *namaste* but did not address a word to anyone else. To my surprise, rather than expecting to be served by Sunni Devi, he helped himself to his food, washed his *thali* (a metal plate with a lip) and then left. He was off to supervise the clipping of his sheep, camped in the wood above the village. Sunni Devi sat back.

'My life is very difficult. I am too much alone. I had another son – so much work children are – and then he died. He was thirteen. And this year my sister died; she was eighteen. She had just been married; she died in a day.' She drew in her breath and pulled her cotton headcloth towards her eyes, preparing herself to cry. I realized it would be improper for her to mention the recent death of such a close relation without wailing. The conversation was getting out of my depth. I said I had to go as Karma and Tchering would be waiting to eat; because I had difficulty in understanding her, and she me. She does not speak or understand much Hindi but she can speak Kangri. So afterwards when I visited her, which I often did, I used to have to persuade Karma or Tchering to come with me to translate through Kangri into Hindi. It was not easy for them as she spoke so softly and confidentially.

Our camp was still where we had pitched it the night before, beside the mulberry tree. It had been late in the afternoon by the time we had struggled up the hill and reached Deori. We had found Pal Singh's house, at the far end of the village, without difficulty. He was the uncle of a shepherd we had met in the Uhl valley, and for whom we had promised to deliver messages.

A *charpoi* (bedstead) had been brought out into the court-yard and spread with a check blanket. Then, in spite of my protestations, tea had been prepared. The *chulha* had been out (everyone is out at work during the day), so it took time to boil the water, and a goat had to be milked before there was milk for the tea. Meanwhile we were offered little sweet-sour peaches and cucumbers served with a green chutney, made of chillis ground with salt – stingy and surprisingly thirst-quenching. As the sun began to lose its warmth, the village became busy. Girls swore at homecoming cattle; women carrying bundles of fodder three times their size staggered into the courtyards; snotty toddlers, tired and hungry, were carried home on an older brother's or sister's back; and men rested their wooden ploughs against the door jamb and called for live charcoal to light their hookahs. And then it was time to move inside, from the courtyard into the kitchen.

Pal Singh was the kind of man you would not notice in a group or a crowded room. He purposely went about his own business or sat silently, rarely entering into general conversation – perhaps it was the effect of his wife's recent death. It was not until I began to talk to him that I realized he had a very definite character and tremendous gentleness. Others in Deori were more overt or enthusiastic in their friendship towards me but I became fond of Pal Singh and respected his reserved wisdom.

47

Throughout our stay in Deori we continued to camp beside his house, partly because I liked him and liked its position, on its own, up round the corner beyond the spring – the rest of the houses are built close together, on either side of the path that runs in an L-shape from the spring down to the temple at the beginning of the village. (Pal Singh has another, larger house in the middle of the village, shaded by old walnut trees and adjoining his brother's.) But also I stayed on there because to continue to be his guest seemed the best hope of not causing misunderstanding or appearing ungrateful to my other friends. For the warmth of the welcome here became embarrassing. Sunni Devi, who became my best friend, begged me, clinging to my clothes, to stay with her. The schoolmaster courteously invited me to stay at his 'humble home' – it was by far the most well appointed in the village. And the *pradhan* (the headman), Pal Singh's brother, summoned me from his veranda with a commanding wave.

I do not know a more perfect view than that from Pal Singh's veranda. It is framed by the wooden arches. The mulberry is in the foreground and, beyond it, small apple and pear trees grow on the edge of the terraces. There at dawn an old woman would gather juicy bits of fodder for the house-goats. Then the terracing falls steeply away so that your gaze moves to the opposite side of the Ravi valley – the north-facing side. There the horizontal light from the rising sun defines the contours of the terracing: a web-like pattern dotted with the stunted shapes of pollarded oak, cut earlier in the spring for fodder.

At the beginning of June the terraces across the middle of the hill were green with unripe wheat and barley, while those lying above and below were brown; only recently planted with maize. Above the terracing the hillside is forested, looking almost black before the sun strikes it. Above the forests are pale green alps – there wispy trails of smoke revealed several shepherds' camps. Higher again is a great sweep of unsullied whiteness, a massive, undulating glacier; as this is the north face of the Dhaula Dhar, the summer's sun never melts the snow. And yet higher, cutting into the azure sky, is a well-shaped peak. It is not cruel or awesome but on a scale that somehow completes the view. The whole seems perfectly composed: to gaze at it is absolute contentment.

In the evening, leaning against the balustrade, sipping a brass beakerful of sweet, goaty tea, I reflected that, if I were asked on my death-bed whether there was anything I wanted, like the Moghul Emperor Jehangir who sighed 'Only Kashmir' I would cry 'Only the view from Deori'.

Within Deori few people have any concept of their origin. Those that do have different versions of it. It was cold standing on Pal Singh's veranda, but the iridescent light on the glacier was so beautiful I was loath to leave and go to my tent.

'What do you mean, where did we come from? We were always here in Gadderan,' Pal Singh said, and he echoed the story Ram Lal had told of how out of Lord Shiva's dirt the flock was created, in order to beat a path across the pass for the gods and how the honour of shepherding the flock had been given to the Gaddis. 'That's why our country is called Shivbhumi, Shiva's land. Shivji gave us our home and our *dharma*. That was in the beginning. That's why, like him, at Shivratri in the month of Phagun, we and our flocks begin to come home for the summer, and in the winter we move south. Mount Kailash and Manimahesh are where we give thanks to him, don't you know?' I asked if he was going there this year. 'No, it is on the way to Lahoul and this year I can't go to Lahoul with the flock. My wife died and I must stay and perform the ceremonies. Next summer I will go and I will perform a *puja* for her at Manimahesh.'

The schoolteacher has a different story about the Gaddis' origin. He lives at the opposite end of the village to Pal Singh. His house is situated at a little distance from his nearest neighbour and secluded by its own orchard. It has electricity: a naked bulb dangled from the veranda. Mr Chauhan is a Gaddi, but as he does not keep flocks or cattle there are living quarters on the ground floor of his house rather than byres and goatherds. He is a well-groomed middle-aged man, very dignified. A lot of people seemed to live at Mr Chauhan's house. His old mother welcomed me with a courteous pride, disturbing herself for a moment from bending over a basket tray, cleaning husk and stones out of beans or grain. And his courtyard was busy with more children than possibly could be his wife. His wife, who was pregnant and looked worn and tired, brought tea and then disappeared.

Mr Chauhan's story of where the Gaddis came from emphasized the significance of the *dora*, the coils of black wool that Gaddi men, women and children wear round their waists. 'We used to be in Lahore, in the Punjab. During the time of the Moghul Aurangzeb they tore the sacred threads off those of us who wore them,[1] and threw them on to a fire. On the fire of burning sacred threads they made tea for Aurangzeb. "Now you are all Muslims," they told us. Some people didn't mind. Those of us who cared fled and we came here, to Bramour. But there was no cultivatable land here, nothing. What were we to do? So the Brahmins sat and recited the *Gayatri*. After some time there was an answer to their prayers – a *dora* appeared. We could not understand. What could be the meaning of the rope? We didn't know. Was it for carrying baggage? For pulling a sheep out of rocky crevasses? Then suddenly it was clear to us: it meant that we were to be shepherds. That is why all Gaddis wear it; it doesn't matter whether you have flocks or not, it is what we wear. It must be as black as possible. I wear it when I go to marriages or festivals.'

The *dora* is twenty to twenty-five yards long. It has no end: it is a circle which is wound round the waist two coils at a time. Mr Chauhan explained how it is made: 'First five strands of spun wool are loosely twisted, then rubbed between your hands. This thickish strand is looped into a crocheted chain and five strands of it are rubbed between the palms of your hands. It is soaked in a trough of water for a day or two. While it is soaking the women tread it with their bare feet. Finally it is rubbed again. It becomes felted and very strong, also very heavy; a new one weighs two and a half kilograms.'

Encouraged by my interest he called for his ceremonial *chola* (the kilted cloak). The tweed (54 feet of 14-inch cloth is needed for a *chola*) was finer and lighter than the cloth of the shepherds' everyday wear. Embroidered in a line round the back, and over the shoulders as well as on the lapels, were minute rosettes. He coiled the *dora* round his waist and then neatly folded the pleats of the *chola*, for the kilted effect. Finally he completed his sartorial elegance by tying a white turban on his head and hanging two brightly coloured medallions from his *dora*.[2] I noticed that the framed portraits were not of his unassuming wife, but of a Bombay movie heroine.

Though I myself have never seen a *dora* being used to pull a sheep out of a crevasse, I have been told stories of how an animal has been rescued with one. Its length and strength ensure that it would be more than adequate. It is useful, too, for other purposes: when it is cold, as a cummerbund, for instance, to keep the stomach and the small of the back warm. Shepherds use it as a pillow; it is good insulation from the cold ground and easy to settle to a comfortable angle – I have slept very comfortably with my head resting on one. Whether Mr Chauhan's story of its appearance in answer to the Brahmins'

51

prayer is really the origin of its importance, for Gaddis it certainly is a symbol of their 'Gaddi-ness' and has a significance beyond its purely practical uses. During the Gaddi marriage ceremony, the bridegroom pretends to set off to become an ascetic (as in the traditional Hindu ceremony); at this moment he shoulders a pack and must be wound into a *dora*. And for a year after the death of her husband, as evidence of her mourning, a widow must wear a belt of natural-coloured goat hair instead of her usual *dora*.[3]

The reason there are so many children at the schoolmaster's house is that relations use it as a hostel for school-age children. Because of their migratory life the children's education has often been intermittent. During the winter some do go to school in Kangra. Mr Chauhan explained that, now people are increasingly concerned about education, families try to arrange for at least one person from the household to stay at home here to look after their schoolchildren. But it is not easy to find teachers who are willing to stay here throughout the winter. Few locals qualify as teachers and those few who do want to get away; while teachers from the towns and plains are reluctant to remain in remote villages, particularly during the long winter.

Mr Chauhan's school caters for children from three villages; it is a primary school with sixty pupils. He has one assistant. The middle and high school is 1500 feet down and four miles miles away at Holi. 'Nowadays, as shepherding is getting more difficult and we are too far from a market here to grow fruit and potatoes for sale, people do want their children to go to school so that they can try to get jobs. Girls, too. Not so many of them go on to middle school because they are needed at home. Also it is a big expense for the family, and who knows after all that expense whether they will get a job?'

'The Nomads [Gaddis and Gujars – the buffalo people] are still at a very inconvenient distance from even a nodding acquaintance with literacy,' wrote T. S. Negi, ex-Speaker of the Himachal Assembly.[4] In an effort to improve the lot of the historically underprivileged, the Indian Constitution listed certain people as 'Scheduled Castes and Tribes' – the sections of society who were considered backward. Gaddis based in Chamba district (Gadderan is part of Chamba) are 'listed'. Among the benefits they receive is a subsidy towards books and clothes for children attending primary, middle and high school.[5] But the subsidy does not fully cover the expenses involved, or the loss to the family of their children's labour, and those who do complete a school career discover that finding employment is not a necessary consequence to becoming literate.

During the time I spent in Deori I thought about the opinions experts have voiced as to who is a Gaddi and who is not, and I tried to form an opinion of my own by talking to friends there. An ethnographic monograph in 1906 referred to them as a *caste* whose original occupation was keeping sheep and goats.[6] The *Chamba Gazetteer* of 1910 – still regarded by many as the official view – said: 'The Gaddis are a separate *clan* [my italics], and under it are included Brahmins, Rajputs, Khatris, Thakurs and Rathis. . . .' J. B. Lyall, the great Gaddi enthusiast, went so far as to say that the Gaddis 'form as it were a distinct *nationality* [my italics]'. And most modern anthropologists consider the Gaddis as a *caste* of lower-caste Rajputs and Khatris.[7] For the average Gaddi there is no issue: he knows who he is, knows to whom he will or will not give his daughter in marriage and with whom he does not share a hookah. Most people I asked would reply, roughly: 'I am a Rajput, I am a Gaddi.'

Throughout northern India there is a new self-consciousness about caste, whereas it used to be unself-consciously accepted. And most of the Gaddis I talked to agreed that caste-consciousness has increased here, too. Pal Singh's view was:

'Before, we didn't know the difference between *kacca khana* and *pakka khana.*' *Kacca khana* means 'uncooked' food, fruit, etc.; it usually includes fried vegetables and types of bread which are fried. *Pakka khana* means chapattis and food cooked with water, including boiled rice. The point of the difference is that *kacca khana* may be regarded as a snack and can be enjoyed sitting beside people by whom you would be polluted if you ate *pakka khana* with them. 'At a wedding feast we all used to sit in a line on the *pangat* – maybe the Brahmins would be put at one end and the Kolis at the other – and we all had a good time. But these days there's a fuss about different sorts of food and who is sitting where.'

Gadderan is not unusual: increasingly the new dimension to caste-awareness has come to regions where previously it hardly existed. From the plains a new terminology has crept into the hills, like *kacca* and *pakka khana*, and there is a modern fashion of giving yourself a title or a recognizably caste surname. Caste distinctions always existed, and were accepted and assumed: the new self-consciousness has been encouraged by politics.[8] Democracy and modern politicians encourage elections fought along caste affinities – 'Vote for me: I am of your caste, of your caste group.'

'. . . Caste which previously played only a minor role in the State's [Himachal's] politics, has become a factor in the remote villages . . . every candidate has a detailed analysis of the caste composition of his constituency in order to play one caste against the other.'[9] And for Gaddis, too, the issue of caste becomes most important in politics, and during elections. Gadderan is a 'reserved' constituency, which means that only a Gaddi may stand as a candidate for the Assembly elections; the theory is to protect the local interests and represent local grievances. But recently a 'Gaddi' from a shop-keeping family living in Chamba town fought and won the Gadderan seat. Some claimed that his win was not valid as he was not a real Gaddi; his family had been shop-keepers for several generations.

Theories about 'Gaddi-ness' seem to me to remain inconclusive, but I feel that Lyall's view of them as a 'nation' has a point. Leaving aside conventional caste taboos about who marries whom and who can eat or smoke with whom, there is within Gadderan, and among its people who have spilled over into Kangra, an affinity which comes from a cultural bond; probably a result of a geographical seclusion. People isolated from others because of their remote terrain develop an affinity less likely to occur on a plain. It of course includes a cultural cohesion – shared deities and festivals, and therefore songs and music. And it helps to explain why the lower castes who live in the area, like the Lohars and Sipis, who have never been regarded as proper Gaddis, also wear the distinctive *chola* and *dora*.

The *pradhan* of the village was more extrovert than his younger brother, Pal Singh. He was a burly man and something of a character. He found me a great joke. Recently he had had his moustaches dyed red and someone had given him a particularly garish Kului cap. 'Don't I look good? Come on, come on. You want to know about Gaddis, who we are? When we first came here? I'll show you; come along with me to an old place.' I was led along some way beyond and above the schoolmaster's house to a crooked, tumbledown semi-ruin. 'See how old it is? So old the stone itself is rotten.'

He gave the stone door jamb a kick and bits of it flaked off: certainly time and weather had taken their toll. He forced me to go into the dark, bat-stinking interior to see just how decrepit were the upstairs floorboards.

'We Gaddis fought in the Mahabharat – there were *jungli* people living here in those days – then we came here.' I was not sure whether he was attributing an age of three thousand years to the 'old' house, or merely settling the question of how long Gaddis have been in Gadderan. 'The *pandas* [learned Brahmins] tell us we came from Lahore, but how do we know if they are telling the truth?'

In any event he considered the issue settled and led me, by the hand, back down the hill. 'Come and see my new English-style house; it will soon be finished, ready for you to stay in next time you come. The glass is in the windows.' Casualties to the glass, bought in Chamba town, transported along the hill road by truck, then reloaded on to a jeep and finally carried up the 1500 feet, must have doubled its purchase price long before the window panes were in place.

Fortunately the glazing was the only concession I could see to the much boasted 'English' style. The house was in fact traditionally built and very well, too; though there was some decorative detail and carving yet to be added to the veranda and its arches.

Standing on his new veranda, he clicked on an electric switch, proudly, as though turning on the Blackpool illuminations: the single bulb glowed a dim yellow. This newly arrived electricity came from a long way off, but he claimed that as *pradhan* he was furthering the cause of a proposed scheme to dam the *nala* running through Deori for a hydro-electric project. 'It will be good work for everyone in the village and then the electricity will be stronger and it won't go off so much.' I thought of the mess and desecration round the Binwa hydel project and was appalled at the prospect, even on a smaller scale, of such squalor here. With difficulty I kept my reactionary romanticism to myself.

I often visited Sunni Devi's house. I became very fond of her gentle sadness, and for some reason she was delighted by our friendship. I found it hard to guess her age. When she smiled, which was not often, her face would slowly light up and she looked hardly more than thirty. In repose, with her more usual expression of the sadness of the world pressing behind her well-set eyes, she might have been ten or fifteen years older. Her figure bore signs of being pregnant at least the four times accounted for. When I asked her how old she was she said, 'My son would have been eighteen or more by now, and I must have been seventeen at my marriage, mustn't I?' I showed her a photograph of my children and took photographs which I promised to bring next time. She gave me a blanket, I gave her a Timex watch. She was overwhelmed as she opened it; she glowed with astonished delight, made me put it on her and wanted to pay me. I reminded her of the huge blanket she had given me. 'That was nothing, that was from the house, our own work. You see, money is very difficult'; and lowering her voice to an almost inaudible whisper, she confided, 'He drinks. All the money we should have, he drinks it. Does your husband drink, too? It's very difficult when they do. He goes off to Lahoul with the sheep and when he comes back there is no money. Every day he must be drinking Lahouli *arak*.'

Our intimacy was interrupted by the arrival of the neighbours from upstairs. Their ten-year-old daughter was admonished for not replying to my *namaste*. 'She doesn't know about it, she has never been to Kangra where you learn these things. Here it is just "*Ram, Ram*" and you answer "*thik, thak*".' The watch was taken out of its box again, to be shown off.

The photographs when developed were intensely puzzled over; for those unused to pictorial representation it takes a few minutes to make out a likeness. They were turned on their sides and upside down and peered into. Tiresome though Sunni Devi finds her sister-in-law, for my sake she asked her for a favour – a packet of *biris*. I had run out and the only *biri-*

and tobacco-seller in the village had gone down to Holi to try to persuade the doctor to come and look at his sick son. The sister-in-law fetched a bundle from upstairs and she and I lit up. Sunni Devi, embarrassed, refused. Then she asked, as though one thing naturally led to the other, did I drink and would I like some *arak*? I did not want her to think of me as belonging in her husband's category, and as it was only ten in the morning I chose instead goat's-milk tea and spinach with maize chapattis.

Two women came in: a girl of about eighteen and her aunt. The relations from upstairs gave them space to sit in our circle. The girl knelt down facing me and took from inside her bodice two pieces of dirty, damp rag. Then, very gently, she lifted out first one breast then the other. They were enormous, shining because they were so distended, the nipples enlarged and almost pulsating with pain. Her eyes were red with the agony and, no doubt, from tears. She had a three-week-old baby, her first, and had been unable to feed it since yesterday. It was acute mastitis or abscesses.

The *dai* (a local woman who gets a reputation for being good at midwifery) who had helped at the delivery had told her to bathe the breasts in leaves soaked in warm water with salt and ash. But the fiery infection was too much for the potion. I was able to give her something for the pain and a course of penicillin I had with me. I was appalled at her suffering, but I was more worried about the baby. There were no bottles or teats, and in the long term a bottle-fed baby somewhere like this, where milk supplies are unreliable and ideas of infection non-existent, would in any case be highly at risk. I had a feeling that the idea of its being wet-nursed would be taboo. I asked the aunt if anyone in the family, a sister or sister-in-law, had a child she was still feeding. Yes, there was one. I asked, gingerly, whether perhaps she could feed the baby for a day or two? She looked horrified at the idea. 'Oh no, we don't do that.' The best I could suggest was boiled water mixed with boiled goat's or cow's milk to be given to the baby from a spoon, and a little breast-milk, too, if the poor girl could manage to express any – I hoped that the penicillin-tainted milk would not upset it.

But that was not to be the end of my medical experiences that day. 'The *biri-wallah* said would I take you to see their boy,' Sunni Devi announced. 'I told them you didn't have medicines, but you have. Will you come there?' I had very few drugs with me and was unnerved at the idea of being considered an expert, but it seemed churlish not to go.

The *biri*-seller's house was at the L-bend in the village, opposite the *pradhan*'s. I was led into an airless room, even darker than usual as the shutters on the windows had been closed. The room seemed full of people. Brusquely I asked for the shutters to be opened, so that I could see and to let in some fresh air. A middle-aged man, who I assumed was the grandfather, introduced me to a round rubbery man, a respected *vaidya* (doctor trained in Ayurvedic medicine). I was told he came from a village down the valley.

The invalid, a boy of five or six, was lying under layers of blankets on a *charpoi*. The *vaidya* told me he thought the child had a chronic kidney complaint and at the moment a dysentery infection, too. He had made his diagnosis largely by feeling the child's pulse (good *vaidyas* are able to diagnose many subtleties of disorder through the pulse), and he had also assessed the puffy face and ankles. He was not in the least antagonistic to me nor did the grandfather seem to anticipate any potential clash between the medical systems of the Orient and the Occident. The dysentery should be cleared, the *vaidya* suggested, before any attempt was made to deal with the kidney disorder. He prescribed powders – two different ones to be taken now and another in a few days when the child was better. He had ground them himself so knew they were pure, from herbs he had collected and from others that had had to be brought from the plains. Then in a week or two, he said, the boy should be brought to him again. He exuded a quiet optimism about the patient that I found difficult to share. We all sat having tea. Wasn't I going to give any medicine? the grandfather asked. He would pay. He wanted good, expensive medicine for this, his only grandson. He did not mistrust the *vaidya*, but he was clutching at any chance. I felt far from confident enough to make any pronouncement, particularly in the presence of the *vaidya*'s expertise. My only suggestion was some fresh air and plenty of boiled water with a little salt and sugar, as much as the boy could be persuaded to take. But I heard later that he did die, two or three weeks afterwards.

I visited Deori again several times after this journey. On the last occasion I came down from the mountains to the north of the village. It was late in the evening by the time we arrived. That day Tchering and I had struggled down a goat track for 6000 feet and misjudged how long it would take. It was already dusk when we reached a village that was still some way above Deori. From a cluster of houses clear, melodious voices sang out across the valley (this time it definitely was not Radio Simla). It seemed a long walk on round the shoulder of the hill towards Deori. By now there were no cow-girls driving their recalcitrant beasts along the path: they were all home. We fixed our eyes on the increasingly indistinct wall-less shelter for travellers that we knew marked the ridge above Deori. And when we reached it we sank our loads against its stone resting bench and wearily smoked a *biri* in silence. After the clear definition of its features in the day's bright sunlight, the Ravi valley was suddenly dark and colourless. We somehow managed to stumble on downhill; our toes bashed against loose stones and our already aching ankles and knees were jarred by the irregularities on the path, invisible in the dark. Again there was that clear, romantic sound of women singing in answering verses. Was it the marriage season in the upper Ravi? Then, at last, through the scanty deodar forest we saw a few indistinct yellow lights – Deori.

We flung our packs on Pal Singh's stone balustrade – coming in on this path from above the village, his house is the first. 'Anyone here?' we called, and climbed the wooden steps, startling two white kids penned on the upper veranda. As thankfully we undid our dusty boots, Pal Singh opened the heavy kitchen door, letting out a slice of orange light. 'Oh, ho ho! It's you!' (He had no idea I was anywhere in Gadderan.) 'Come in, come in. Where have you come from at this time of night?' He grasped my right hand between his two palms (none of the 'touch-me-not' *namaste*), led me in and spread a goat-hair mat for us by the *chulha*. His daughter-in-law quickly took the girdle off the fire and put in its stead the round brass water-vessel to boil for tea. 'Bring some wood for light,' Pal Singh called, and a boy took some embers from the fire and, with tongs, carefully placed them on a chimney-shaped clay lamp-stand above the fire. The pieces of wood which he put on top of the embers burst into flame. (Bits of resinous pine wood are used as torches outdoors and as lights indoors.) It was not exactly that the lighting of the lamp was an extravagance indulged in only for our benefit, but that before we arrived the firelight had been adequate. The lamp was unnecessary; not enough had been going on.

Now in the warm, flickering circle of its glow I could see who was in the room. An old woman, whom I had not met before, was Pal Singh's aunt. She had walked up from her village, 1500 feet below, to visit and was spending the night. She clicked her tongue loudly against the roof of her mouth to express her sympathy with our weariness. Out of the pouch in the bodice of her dress she took two large apples, and, holding the kitchen sickle between her toes, cut the fruit into perfectly even sections. The boy there was Gunu, a ten-year-old grandson. The two white kids had profited by the excitement of our arrival and taken the chance to escape from the veranda pen into the warmth of the kitchen. Gunu was cuddling and teasing them. His soft face and worn tweed jacket and their velvety skin absorbed the mellow light – it might have been a Rembrandt illustration of a story from the Bible.

Usha Devi, the daughter-in-law, had been busy outside the circle of light, over by a low clay shelf where the pots were kept. She beckoned me to the side of the room, and to my astonishment – it took me a moment to appreciate what she was about to do – took my foot and placed it in a copper vessel of salty hot water. She massaged first one foot, then the other, pressing the aching tiredness down and squeezing it away. It was an incredible sensation of pleasure, and what a generous expression of hospitality! She opened a shuttered window to throw out the slops: suddenly there appeared a rectangle of white light. I could not understand. Then I realised it was moonlight reflected off the steep bank on the far side of the *nala*, a mere fifty feet away. There was no sky to see, for the bank was far higher than the house. Then she attended to Tchering's feet.

Pal Singh explained that the singing we had heard was not because of a marriage, neither here nor at the village above: it was because of a festival marking the first day of the new month. And in celebration Usha Devi had been cooking special chapattis, not the usual thin flat ones but a leavened variety. Having given us our reviving tea, she replaced the water-pot with the iron *tawa* and pushed some embers into a corner of the fire. Then, aiming at the heart of the fire, she gently blew through a hollow tube of bamboo – a precious utensil brought from Kangra as no large bamboos grew here. When each circle of dough was seared on both sides she pulled it off the *tawa* with her fingers and laid it on the hot embers in the corner. The heat blew it up into a sphere, and, now fully fired, it was put with the others, tucked underneath a cloth in a basket. Before she had finished all the prepared dough she must have made thirty or forty chapattis.

Soothed by the comfort of warm tired limbs, rested and lulled by the bubble of Pal Singh's hookah, I felt myself withdrawing. I began to look at the circle of people in the gentle light and shadows as though from a distance. At last, just as I was dozing off, Usha Devi was ready to serve food. Though while our feet were being tended we had also washed our hands, we were given a dish in which to wash them again before eating (a formal Hindu convention not often practised by hill people). We gorged ourselves on the chapattis, freshly harvested *rajma dal*, black *ma dal*, tomato chutney and jam (slices of apple added to boiled sugar and water). The food was served on gleamingly clean, brass *thalis*.

That night we had no tent and I slept on the veranda. In the village they were still singing:

> O Shivji if you grant my desires,
> Eighty goats and eighty-four sheep
> I will give you if you fulfil my desires.
> Eighty threads, if you agree,
> A red flag – I will get it coloured –
> On that flag I will also sprinkle blood.[10]
> I will give drink, too,
> I will sing you shepherds' songs
> If I find that my desires are fulfilled,
> Open-hearted I will receive you.
> The month of Sawan[11] is coming,
> I must go, I must go.
> O Shivji, if you give me your *darshan*
> I will do all these things.

Before I sank into sleep, I glowed in appreciation of the warmth of our welcome. Though I have spent relatively little time in Deori I feel a friendliness there I have never felt in Kulu, where I have lived for many years. There I have seldom been offered more than a casual cup of tea on the veranda and never been invited inside anyone's kitchen. I do not know why Kuluis' attitude to outsiders should be so different from that of Gaddis. I do not think it is that Kuluis, from over-exposure to foreigners, have become indifferent to them; for the Kului villagers of the higher, more remote valleys are no more forthcoming. Nor is it that Kuluis are constrained by ideas of 'uncleanliness' while Gaddis are not: in fact rather the opposite is true. Kuluis have a relatively easy-going attitude to the conventional taboos; Gaddis are more meticulous about observing the niceties of ritual and avoiding pollution – like always washing before eating. I noticed, too, when we stood on the veranda for an after-dinner smoke that Pal Singh did not offer Tchering a draw on his hookah (though shepherds out in the hills sometimes do, first removing the mouthpiece so that it must be sucked through your clenched fist).

Logically it is the Gaddis who should be more circumspect towards outsiders. They are more conventional Hindus than most people in these hills; this was as true a hundred years ago, when Lyall wrote, 'The Gaddis wear the thread of caste and are much stricter in Hindu customs and observances than most inhabitants of the higher ranges of the Himalayas.' They are also unusual in their devotion to a deity who belongs to the central Hindu pantheon – Lord Shiva. I have found no convincing answer to the question of why they are comparatively orthodox Hindus and such staunch Shaivites. Maybe it has to do with where they came from and who they were before they moved from the plains to the shelter of the remote hills.

I found it difficult to come to conclusions as to the whys

and wherefores of how Gaddis see themselves, because they do not have an objective view of themselves. Even the questions I tried to ask were meaningless to them. So the answers were apt to be something like – 'How do you mean, why do we worship Lord Shiva? He looks after us so we have always worshipped him.' People do not know why they perform sacrifices to one deity and not to another whom they revere equally. Nor why they perform ceremonies in a different way from their neighbours. And, of course, every time I asked a question I got a different answer. The only way to gather some understanding is by watching and listening. And then it is almost irresistible to weave a pattern from what you have learnt, to interpret what you see and hear and to contrive the material into a cogent argument. The danger is that after some time you let yourself believe that your theory is more than a subjective opinion.

I was having a very enjoyable time in Deori, but Karma and Tchering were becoming restless, tired of translating for me and Sunni Devi, and it was time that we moved on. Pal Singh's flock had already left, to spend two weeks on the hill up above, before moving on north, and Sunni Devi's husband was setting off in a few days' time by a high route, above Bramour. We were to take the lower route as I wanted to spend a little time in Bramour, the old capital of Chamba and Gadderan's headquarters.

Leaving Deori was embarrassing. Usha Devi, Pal Singh's daughter-in-law, gave me tomatoes and peaches, and Pal Singh himself filled my haversack with potatoes. Then, when I went to say goodbye to Sunni Devi, she made me sit and have tea and in the meantime scuffled about in her chests filling *thalis* full of *rajma* and *ma dal* and maize flour, and bringing out a carefully hidden clothful of walnuts. Every bag I had was already jammed and all my pockets, too. There are no paper or plastic bags in the village, so the *dals* had to be tied into opposite ends of my scarf and the walnuts into an end which she ripped off her own headcloth. I left, with a cucumber in my hand, embracing her first over her right then over her left shoulder and begging her to come down to where we would be camped beside the river – we had to buy rations from the bazaar at Holi. She said she would be too shy.

But she did come down that evening. For company, and probably to give her support, she brought a stalwart, almost fat, woman, whose chin tattoos were the blackest and the most intricately defined of any I have seen. They sat to the side of our kitchen fire. Sunni Devi had brought a *dora* for me. (I had asked if anyone in the village had one to sell, as I had a *luanchari* but no *dora*.) Of course she would not take any money. They both took a *biri* but each smoked with it well hidden in the palm of her hand. Every now and then they glanced up at the path through the trees above, lest the revellers, coming back from a wedding up the valley, might notice their immodesty. Sunni Devi was in no hurry to leave. She was intrigued by the paraphernalia of our camp and I think she was loath to accept that our friendship was about to be interrupted for an unknown length of time.

We exchanged addresses and promised to write to each other. It was her idea, and sitting on the sand there by the river it seemed an ordinary thing to do. But months later when I came to write to her I felt it was improbable that my envelope would ever reach her. Finally, when it was getting dark, she stood up and took from inside the bodice of her dress two white eggs which she gave me. Then they left, often turning to look back at us. By the time they would have crossed the river it was too dark to see them climbing up the zig-zag path back to Deori.

Deep inside me I treasure my friendship with Sunny Devi

and the beauty of Deori. Though I can seldom go there I often think about it. If I found out that suddenly something had happened and she and the village did not exist, I would feel the loss for ever.

1. The thread worn over the chest and shoulder by high-caste Hindu men.

2. Men's medallions are called *gharat chatta*; those of the women are called *chiri*.

3. P. R. Phillimore, 'Marriage and Social Organisation among Pastoralists of the Dhaula Dhar'.

4. T. S. Negi, *Scheduled Tribes of Himachal Pradesh*.

5. Primary-, middle- and high-school children are given 8, 12 or 15 rupees per month respectively, and receive 30, 50 or 80 rupees per year towards books and clothes. There are no school fees for state education in India. Gaddis based in Kangra do not receive the scheduled caste and tribe benefit. The anomaly may be because Kangra was a part of the old Punjab and has only recently been included in Himachal state, or that Gaddis based there were considered to be better off. Or it may be that Gaddis in Kangra, when completing census details, have always entered themselves as Rajputs rather than as Gaddis.

6. Edmund O'Brien and M. Morris, *The Kangra Gaddis*.

7. It is more or less established that no Gaddi Brahmin will give his daughter to a Rajput or a Khatri Gaddi – with the possible exception of Brahmins living in Kugti, where certainly until recently Brahmins did intermarry with others. A Gaddi Brahmin is much more likely to marry his daughter to a Kangra Brahmin than to a Gaddi non-Brahmin. Similarly Rajput or Khatri Gaddis, who do not regard the people of Barabangahal (away at the top of the Ravi valley) as Gaddis, do sometimes marry their daughters into Bangahali families – though I think such an agreement is rather disparaged.

8. The practice of having to state your caste when giving information for the *Census and Gazetteers*, initiated by the British, is still continued. The caste basis of every constituency can be readily assessed from the census returns.

9. *India Today*, 31 May 1982.

10. From the sacrifice of the goats and sheep.

11. The rainy season.

CHAPTER THREE

Bramour, the Old Capital

Early summer

I had imagined Bramour might have a comfortable hotel and at least plenty of luxuries like vegetables, eggs and bread, and busy cafés. As we walked down the Ravi valley, Karma, Tchering and I had talked about hot *pakora* and plates of meat and steaming rice. It was almost dusk when we arrived. I sat grumpily on a stone platform drinking a glass of tea made with dried milk and eating a stale sweet. Schoolchildren were playing hopscotch and marbles in the dust.

At the entrance to the village the track passed local government offices – the usual dishevelled, dozy buildings roofed with standard Public Works Department corrugated iron. As Bramour is at 7000 feet, snow had taken its toll and a good many of the roofs were battered. The cobbled track led on up past an English wine shop and through the bazaar – a silversmith's, two or three cloth shops, a grain store and a couple of scruffy tea hotels – into the main square.

It was not until the next morning that I realized that the stone platform where I had sat disconsolately drinking my tea was in fact the famous *Chaurasi* (eighty-four) – the main square which owes its name to the eighty-four shrines built there. Some are merely four-foot-high cones sheltering *lingams* – the phallic symbol of Lord Shiva. Goats and sheep were trying to squeeze their way inside the shrines to benefit from the cool shade. Other flocks and their shepherds, all on their way north for the summer, were resting in the shade of the walnut trees. A very large stone temple in the classical style dominates the square: the Manimahesh temple, sacred to Lord Shiva. In front of it, under a sheltering roof but otherwise open, is a life-size, standing bull – Nandi. This brazen bull looked so life-like and so dazzlingly shiny that I found it hard to believe that it was the famous statue which dates Bramour's first glorious era to have been in the late seventh century. Its pedestal has an inscription attributing the work to the crafts-man Gugga, in the reign of Raja Meru Varman (AD 680–700). This was the raja who put Bramour on the map of North India, and the beautiful images still in the temples were due to his inspiration.

The Lammergeier, or Bearded Vulture, in the Himalayas flies higher than any other bird. With its nine-foot wingspan, circling in the air currents at 24,000 feet, it looks down over Gadderan on a bewildering complexity of mountains and valleys. It might well wonder why men moved north from the well-watered plains of Hindustan, and moved on from the com-paratively domesticated hills of Kangra. For, from high above, it must seem absurd that men would want to cross the Dhaula Dhar, to settle somewhere where narrow terraces cling to steep and inhospitable mountainsides, only just below the early summer's snow-line. The sun shimmers on the virgin snow of the summits. Glaciers groan as they inch forward. Their gaping green chasms are reminiscent of the enchanted world of a gothic fairy tale, while the moraine around them creates a surprisingly sordid scene; the mud, rocks and dirty snow resemble a rubbish dump. Rivers, deep in their gorges, are forced by mountain massifs to flow in the opposite direction to their ultimate goal; taking great turns and loops before stretching out to flow, like flat ribbons, across the blue plains. Hillsides are gashed by landslides; rocks, trees and soil have slid away.

The vegetation is inconsistent: ridges are treeless on one side while the other is forested and dark green. And if you were able to look down from the Lammergeier's vantage point, high above Mount Kailash, you would be puzzled: if immigrants moved up from the plains, why isn't there a progressive pattern of villages and cultivation? To the south-east there are green and pleasant-looking hillsides that are uncultivated; while far to the north isolated hamlets, and their surrounding patchwork of cultivation, perch on humps of moraine left by receding glaciers. There are some logical reasons for this seemingly arbitrary scatter of settlements: south-facing slopes are pale green and treeless because the winter and early-spring sun melts the snow, so that not enough moisture is retained for trees, let alone cultivation. Then there is the net effect of altitude on crops; the higher the altitude, the shorter the growing season. But the maximum possible height for cultivation does vary from place to place. In Kangra the highest fields and villages are at a mere 5000 feet; in Kulu at 7000 feet; but in Lahoul, the Upper Satlej valley and in Zanskar communities survive off crops grown at 11,000 and 12,000 feet.

The inconsistent pattern of habitation in these mountains is related, too, to the communication routes, or the lack of them. The headwaters of four out of five of the great rivers of the Punjab force their way through this intricate tangle of mountains. They are (from west to east) the Chenab, the Ravi, the Beas and the Satlej (though the last actually rises in Tibet). It might be assumed that these river valleys would be the communication routes, but it is not necessarily so. The ferocious forces of glacier and river have cut such deep gorges through the rock that valley sides are often too precipitous even for a goat track, let alone a path for laden men. In some valleys the torrent has been unfordable and unbridgeable for centuries, isolating one bank from the other. It may be almost impossible to reach a village which is just along the valley, or on the other side of the river, and easier to reach another lying across a mountain pass of 16,000 or 17,000 feet; often under snow for many months of the year.

Men penetrated into the mountains thousands of years ago, and, from different directions, have continued to do so in waves ever since. They all left their original homes for similar reasons: they felt threatened. It might have been that grazing became inadequate; more often, they were fleeing from political or religious persecution. (Some individuals left home because they chose to meditate in the peace and solitude of the mountains, known to be the home of the gods.) Most came, by one route or another, from the plains of Hindustan, driven by succeeding invaders from the west – Aryans, Muslims, and Mongols. Others came down from the north, from the high, arid plateaux of Central Asia.

Circling in the sky high above you could hardly discern the V of Gadderan. Gadderan is officially known as Bramour *tehsil* (district); Bramour village is the capital. Fifty thousand of the estimated eighty thousand Gaddi people live here; all but a few of the rest live in Kangra. Gadderan consists of the valleys of the Upper Ravi and the Budil rivers, and the mountainous area between. Dominated by Mount Kailash, Shiva's seat, at 18,564 feet, the country is also known as 'Shivbhumi'. It is in the shape of a V lying on its side, with its apex at Karamukh, at the confluence of the Ravi with the Budil. The southern arm of the V is the Ravi valley; from where the river emerges from its gorge near Nayagraon (on the path that we

71

followed down from the Jalsu pass), and on down to Karamukh. The northern arm is the Budil valley, from Karamukh
up past Bramour and beyond.

Looking down on the tangle of wild mountains, it would
seem inconceivable that in the late seventh century, on a
small promontory at Bramour, there had been a flourishing
court. That thirteen centuries ago it had been the seat of an
expansionist raja.

Bramour is seldom visited by outsiders, even Indiologists,
though it is an important historical, archaeological and religious site; for the mountain barriers which used to make it an
attractive refuge continue to isolate it. The journey in by
'motor', as Gaddis call buses, trucks and jeeps, takes so long
that people prefer to walk, the way we had come – over the
Jalsu pass and down the Ravi valley. But the track is not even
fit for mules. Mules can cross the Jalsu, and come to just beyond Tchering's uncle's hotel, but the stretch below, down
to the Ravi itself, is too sheer and the path too precarious for
laden mules. To reach Bramour we had walked on down the
Ravi valley from Holi bazaar. The last ten miles of the way was
called 'jeepable': even by Himachal hill-road standards it was
a dramatic jeep track. In places it was cut under the rock face;
here and there not cut in far enough, so that the outside wheels
skittered along the crumbling 'berm' of the road, from time
to time bouncing in thin air high above the river. Karma and
Tchering eagerly threw their packs into a passing jeep, and
Tchering bravely jumped in, too; I preferred to walk. A
quarter of a mile ahead we caught up with the jeep: the driver
had wisely stopped to make an offering, for safe journey, at
the roadside shrine. There was one at least every mile and all
were well frequented.

We had met the main road, coming in from Chamba, at
Karamukh. The only low-altitude route from the plains to
Chamba comes up the Ravi valley from Pathankot (until the

1960s it was an untarred track). Then from Chamba, for 35 miles up to Karamukh, the road is classed as a 'fairweather road' – a narrow, metalled track, precarious because prone to landslides and dangerous when it rains because of slippery mud and rocks falling from above.

Tchering, with our baggage, and all the passengers off the Chamba bus, were waiting at the tea hotel. Tchering had discovered why: Karamukh is the end of the road for the bus coming in from Chamba; the bridge across the Ravi is too narrow for buses or trucks. All passengers, carrying their baggage, must walk across the bridge and wait for the one bus which runs on the eight-mile stretch up to Bramour. Ten years ago, before the bridge was completed with railings, this bus was driven across to spend the rest of its life a prisoner on the far side. I wondered how it would be replaced when the mechanics declared it beyond repair.

When at last it arrived it was obvious that its passengers were all expert at grabbing a seat before it stopped. So for us it was the roof. Every now and then when travelling in the Himalayas you must disregard prudence and accept situations which in normal circumstances you would dismiss as being far too risky; you must conquer apprehension. The driver was in a hurry: we whirled round hairpin bends high above the river and plunged down 1-in-4 gradients like a roller coaster. How tightly I could cling to the 9-inch rail round the bus roof was a question of life and death. And if the brakes or steering failed (I knew that maintenance, so far from work-shops and beyond the end of the road, must be minimal), there would be no survivors. But having had experience of Hima-chali buses I succeeded in suspending all apprehension: the views were magnificent and after so many days on foot the sensation of speed was thrilling.

In Bramour's ancient *Chaurasi*, the sight of shepherds and flocks resting on their centuries-old migratory route to the north was picturesque and arresting. For them the dangers of the mountainous terrain ahead, and the power of the gods who inhabit it, and the realities of wool and meat prices, were more important than theories about the history of the area. But I wanted to try to understand who the Gaddis were and why they came here.

Bramour is unusual. Because of its isolation it was never invaded by iconoclastic Muslims, nor conquered by Gurkhas or Sikhs, nor taken over by the British. Its temples and their images and its court records have remained intact; not vandalized by invaders, as in so much of north India. So experts have been able to put together an unusually authentic history of the state, though parts, particularly for the earlier centuries, remain conjecture.

Historians say that Bramour was founded by a Raja Maru Varman at the end of the sixth century. Raja Maru Varman inherited a kingdom in the Upper Ganges valley. He was a religious man who had devoted his life to prayer and self-mortification. Then suddenly he married and had three sons. When they grew up he decided that they should each have a kingdom. So he gave the family kingdom to the eldest and he and the other two set off to travel across the Punjab. He found a kingdom for the second son in the mountains somewhere near Kashmir. Finally, with the youngest, Jaistambh, he arrived here in the Upper Ravi valley and they founded the state of Brahmapura – Bramour. There is no mention of how they defeated the local barons who must have held the territory. Then later, when the state and its capital were well established, Maru Varman gave it all to the young Jaistambh and he himself travelled back to his original home, where again he devoted himself to religion and self-mortification. The story sounds improbable. Did Raja Maru really believe that the most likely path to salvation for his three sons was that they should rule isolated, unsought-after mountain kingdoms; where, while nominally fulfilling their princely roles, they would have time for reflection and meditation?

There is a local story describing the founding of the capital which echoes the historians' version but, allowing for the licence of legend, makes more sense. Jaistambh was the son of a ruling chief of Rajputana who quarrelled with his father and was expelled from the family kingdom. So the prince decided to renounce the world and become a holy man, a sadhu. During his wanderings, he met a particularly impressive guru who persuaded him that he should give up living as a wandering holy man and instead go back to being a Rajput prince, and directed him towards Bramour. When Jaistambh, once again dressed in princely finery and accompanied by a courtly retinue, arrived at Karamukh, he was welcomed by Rishi Agryachari. The *Rishi* (renowned holy man) had had a vision in which Lord Shiva had described the impending arrival of the prince, and he had been instructed to go and welcome him and to present him with a *topa*, *chola* and *dora* – the symbolic attire of Lord Shiva (and the Gaddis). Then the holy man/prince/personification of Lord Shiva, founded the capital.

Some say that the first Gaddi Brahmins and Rajputs arrived from somewhere near Delhi, two hundred years after Bramour was founded. This was during the reign of Raja Ajia Varman, AD 780–800. He, like his ancestor Maru, the founder, abdicated and devoted his life to the worship of Lord Shiva – his retreat was near Karamukh. The estimated dates of Raja Ajia's reign mean that Gaddis may have been fleeing from the conquest of Delhi and its surroundings by King Lalitiditya of Kashmir. Perhaps Bramour was known as a Shaivite haven, so that if Gaddis were staunch Shaivites it would have been the obvious destination.

Whether in fact they already were Shiva worshippers and therefore felt drawn here, or whether they only began to worship him after they arrived and found that he was the established deity, cannot be proved. To some degree all of the Himalayas are associated with Shiva and his consort Parvati, for these mountains are his home. When the river Ganga threatened the world with its devastating rush out of the mountains, he controlled it by forcing the water to run through his tangled hair. And she, Parvati, is the daughter of Himavat – the personification of the Himalayas. But in certain areas the association with Lord Shiva is particularly strong. Mount Kailash and Lake Mansowar on the Indian–Tibetan border are the most famous; 'Shivbhumi' is another. Whether the Gaddis arrived in Bramour as Shiva-ites or became his followers after arriving here, for them today he is omnipresent, their *dharma*-giver and simultaneously Lord and hero of many of their stories and songs.

Some Gaddis must have arrived in Bramour before the first quarter of the tenth century, because the state annals mention that Gaddi soldiers assisted Raja Sahil Varma (920) in his battles against the Kuluis. This was one of the great eras for the state: when it subjugated parts of Kulu, Lahoul, Kashmir, Kangra and even the Punjab.

The next wave of Gaddis probably arrived at the end of the tenth century or early in the eleventh. By this time much of Sahil Varma's empire had been lost – including Kangra and Kulu. The plains were reeling under the first Mohammedan invasions and refugees were scattering towards the hills. Some Gaddis had retreated from the plains to the shelter of the Kangra rajas. Then when Sultan Mahmud of Gazna attacked Kangra fort and finally succeeded in sacking it in 1009, 'most of them [the Gaddis] seemed to have moved beyond the Dhaula Dhar into Bramour, which since then has become Gaddi country *par excellence.*'[1]

At times of invasions and persecutions (most often from the west), the flow of refugees into the hills increased. It is un-likely that all the members of a clan, caste or group moved simultaneously or immediately established themselves in one place. More probably they scattered: and then over the years or decades, or the next time there was reason to flee, when word had spread that some of their group had found a particularly congenial place, others were drawn there. (It continues to happen today: semi-nomadic Khampa traders from Tibet, who began to look for land from a hundred to fifty years ago, first settled in many places in the West Himalayas; wherever they could get a toe-hold. More recently they have congregated in places where opportunities have favoured them – like Manali and Kulu and the Upper Satlej.) Whenever Gaddis felt threatened and needed to move they remembered hearing that there was a haven for them at Bramour. The last wave of immigration was in the late seventeenth century: the story of how they escaped the zealous Emperor Aurangzeb's persecutions in Lahore is so well known and detailed that there must have been a large number who arrived here then.

Were the Gaddis semi-nomadic sheep-herders before they arrived at Bramour, or did they take to shepherding once here, for lack of any other livelihood? It is no easier to answer this than it is to answer the question of whether they were Shaivites before or became so after they arrived here. Herman Goetz quoted an early, rather vague, reference to their being descendants of the old Gadhaiyas once found in many parts of north-west India, and added, without any detailed information, that 'The Gaddis were a semi-nomadic tribe inhabiting the Punjab, probably Takkasesa, though originally they may have come from the Hindu Kush region, as they have many affinities with the Kafirs.' He pointed out that immigrant refugees coming into the hills would have had to find a livelihood fitting to their social status and tradition; Rajputs and Thakurs could not become cobblers or potters. When cultivatable land was scarce, times when local rajas were fighting were advantageous: the call to arms was an appropriate profession, and to be a mercenary soldier was not demeaning. Gaddis were used by the rajas of Chamba as mercenary soldiers; there is also a later reference to their assistance during the successful re-taking of Lahoul from the Tibetans by Raja Pratab Singh Varman in 1570. In appreciation of their military service they always held a special, elevated position in the rajas' esteem. After the capital had moved to Chamba there was a double coronation. During the second, held at Bramour, the Raja was dressed in ceremonial Gaddi clothes. And if ever there was a dispute Gaddis had immediate redress via the Raja himself. In 1863–4 the British were instrumental in disbanding the Raja of Chamba's private army[2] after which the Gaddis' political power declined, and also their association with military service.

Edmund O'Brien, who studied the Gaddis in the late nineteenth century, wrote that 'the caste believes its original occupation to have been the keeping of sheep and goats and trading in these animals, in their wool and hair, and trading in *charas* (cannabis), camphor and gold with Ladakh. They have also always pursued agriculture, but agriculture has increased of late years, especially the cultivation of rice. They do not take service [take on work for employers], with very few exceptions. They adhere to their original occupation, i.e. that of shepherds and goatherds, traders in the special articles above named and agriculture.'[3]

The village survey on Bramour supports this view of the caste's original occupation : 'The greater portion of the people's wealth is flocks. The other is agriculture. They follow it in a rather indifferent and fitful way on account of their migrations.'[4]

But the anthropologist W. H. Newall, who lived near Bramour for some time, came to quite the opposite conclusion. 'The Gaddis are an agricultural people who take up other occupations from occupational necessity rather than desire.'

And '. . . it is clear that the Gaddis are not principally a sheep caring, nomadic people but have been so for hundreds of years as an additional means of sustenance.'[5]

When I took evening walks around Bramour, up or down the Budil valley, I was struck by the poor quality of the crops. Stunted wheat grew in only one corner of a weedy field and in another the crop was so threadbare that it could be reaped in a few handfuls. Why are Gaddis such poor cultivators? Hillsides are steep, the terraces only two or three yards wide, and the rainfall is unreliable, with a variation of 22.33 to 80.77 inches from one year to another; but these cannot account wholly for their lack of success. The Lahoulis labour under a much more adverse climate and at a much higher altitude; and even the villagers of dry and poor Outer Saraj till more respectable crops. Part of the answer may be that so many of the cultivators migrate south for the winter. Before they leave the winter crop must be hurriedly sown and, untended and unweeded, cannot be expected to give a good yield. But that raises the question: why do they migrate?

From nowhere else, even from villages at comparable heights, is there winter migration on such a large scale. The Gaddis' explanation is that they move south because Lord Shiva does. It seems to me they migrate because they have always been shepherds (perhaps traders, too); for generations they have been in the habit of moving to find pasture for their flocks. For them cultivation of crops is less important than the welfare of those flocks.

My view may be romantic, but I became convinced that, whatever their original occupation, they have looked on shepherding for generations as their *dharma* from Lord Shiva:

> The Gaddis feed their flocks
> The Gaddinis offer incense [to Lord Shiva]
> To the Gaddis He [Shiva] gives sheep
> And to the Gaddinis beauty.

And also:

To an old man do not give me, Father, do not give me, Father,
I shall be a widow while my hair is freshly done.
To a servant do not give me, Father, do not give me, Father,
A call comes; he gets up and goes and leaves me.
To one who lives far away do not give me, Father, do not give me,
    Father,
Give me to one who grazes a herd of beasts.
To a sick man do not give me, Father, do not give me, Father,
I shall become a widow while my hair is still freshly done.
Give me to a herder of sheep, Father, give me, Father,
He will give me his pocket full of meat,
Give me to a tender of sheep, Father, give me, Father,
He will give me a *chola* for my back.[6]

The affection which I saw Gaddis give their sheep and particularly their goats is unusual. It revealed an affinity with their animals seldom expressed by others whose livelihood depends on them; for instance, by a muleteer for his mules. Shepherds breed their handsome mastiff-type dogs with care and feed them well but I never saw them give their dogs even the casual affection a Scots shepherd occasionally does give his working collie. I noticed that Gaddi children played with the kids rather than dogs, and I saw a single sheep walk, day after day, following its owners like a pet. On the plains it is the cows that can wander freely into temples; here in Bramour, both goats and sheep wandered into the temples unchecked. I watched a toddler sitting on its mother's knee picking up and munching a lump of sheep dropping: he was not reprimanded – I assumed it was not considered polluting. At a rest stop while we had been coming down the Ravi valley I had noticed a group of travellers give an offering to a wayside shrine and then share out the *prasad* (an offering: in this case *gur* and chapatti). When one of the men had put it into his mouth, a sheep gave him a nudge on the knee. 'Oh ho!' he said.

'Dear me, you didn't get any' – and he stuck out his tongue for the sheep to lick it off.

All over the West Himalayas animals are sacrificed on festive occasions, or to request a favour from the deity, but none are so conscientious as the Gaddis with their ritual ceremonies, or so generous to the gods with their goats. Goat sacrifice is an intrinsic part of their culture and religion, and goats – and sheep – have a status beyond their economic utility. At the full moon in the month of *Asarha* Gaddis worship the goats and sheep, pray for them and decorate them, honouring their means of livelihood.

A shepherd who was passing time sitting on the stone platform under a walnut tree told me – between long drags on his hookah – a story of how the *Chaurasi* was given its name. It is one of those stories that entwine a powerful indigenous deity with a conventional Hindu one.

'Brahmini Devi lived on the ridge above the village. Her son had a pet partridge. A villager killed the bird and Brahmini's son died of a broken heart. She burnt the bird and also her son and herself. Then for a long time she took her revenge on the Bramouris. They tried to please her by building a temple on the ridge, but still her rage was often and easily roused. When Lord Shiva came with his eighty-four saints, all dressed as though they were pilgrims, on their way up to Manimahesh, they rested here. Brahmini got a whiff of the smoke from their cooking fires and went into a rage because they had camped here without permission. She became the terrifying *Virat Rup* [the manifestation of a horrible monster] and she roared at Shiva and ordered him and his followers to move on. He, humbly, asked for permission to stay for the night. In the morning the eighty-four saints had become eighty-four stone *lingams*. After that, in deference to her power, Lord Shiva granted Brahmini Devi a boon: pilgrims on their way to Manimahesh should first bathe here in the Brahmini pool.'

I became fond of Bramour and its slow pace. I spent time sitting in the *Chaurasi* watching the neatly dressed school-children assembling for the high school behind the Narasimha temple. On the opposite side of the dusty square was an open-fronted temple with a magnificent image of Ganesh (Shiva and Parvati's son), the elephant god. His massive bronze bulk was elevated to fine art by the curve of his trunk, his enormous decorative ears, and by the extraordinary delicacy of his hands.

But to the right and a little set back from the Ganesh was the temple I found the most moving. It is an ignominious construction – small, and from the outside tumble-down; you might easily pass it by. Beyond two dark entrance porches, the image of the *Devi* stands in the shadowy inner sanctuary. As on the pedestal of the brazen bull, an inscription says that this image was cast by the famous artist Gugga. The image is of Lakhna Devi – the powerful deity who had punished the thoughtless shepherd on our way down from the Jalsu pass. Here she has her right foot on a buffalo. In one of her four hands she holds its tail, with another she sticks a trident into the buffalo's neck and in a third she holds a bell. Despite being boss-eyed, she is gracious and very elegant. It is extra-ordinary that such sophisticated beauty was cast in bronze fourteen hundred years ago, in these remote hills. But it was the wood carving on the inside of the two entrance porches, probably contemporary with the image, that I found even more moving: curvaceous figures standing in arched niches, lintels and door jambs demonstrating the flourish of the carver's art, and wonderful, elongated lions. A woman wearing a tattered *luanchari* and I would sit for hours in the dusty shade of the entrance, lost in awe.

*

It was getting hot and sultry: it was mid-June. Like the resting shepherds and their flocks I had to shelter from the midday sun in the temples, or under the walnut trees. Just as the sheep were hungry for the new alpine grass, I wanted to sniff the heady air of the high places. It was time to move on north; to begin the journey into the high hills, towards Lahoul and the summer grazing.

1. Herman Goetz, *Early Wooden Temples of Chamba*.

2. P. R. Phillimore, 'Marriage and Social Organisation among Pastoralists of the Dhaula Dhar'.

3. Edmund O'Brien and M. Morris, *The Kangra Gaddis*.

4. *A Village Survey, Bramour HP*, Census of India 1961, Vol. XX, Part VI, No. 5, ed. Ram Chandra Pal Singh.

5. W. H. Newell, 'Census of India 1961, Vol. XX, Part V-B HP. Report of Scheduled Castes and Scheduled Tribes'.

6. As quoted by M. S. Randhawa, *Farmers of India Vol. 1, Punjab*, HP Jammu and Kashmir.

CHAPTER FOUR

Pilgrimage to Manimahesh Lake
and on into the interior

The terraces of thin, undersized maize and those where the
scanty crop of winter wheat had been recently harvested
stretched only a mile or two up the Budil valley from Bramour.
Beyond, as far as Hadsar (nine miles away), there are no
villages. The path snaked along, sometimes perched on the
cliff-side, sometimes cut into it. On the opposite side of the
river the mountains were almost as steep but less rocky.
Across there, there were a few precarious patches of terracing and the green hillside was cut into endless Z shapes by
sheep and goat tracks. We were walking along the upper arm
of the V of Gadderan, heading north-east, towards Kugti, the
Kugti pass, and ultimately Lahoul.

Reaching the top of two hundred irregular steep steps cut
into the rock and slippery with fresh dung, I stopped, to
regain breath and to look down into the river in its chasm. It
is a wild, romantic valley. Ahead I suddenly noticed a lone
shepherd sitting, smoking a *chilam* (the bowl of a hookah). On
the narrow path beside him there was a ewe. I thought it odd
that both man and sheep were alone. It was not until I began
to negotiate my way round them that I realized the ewe was

lambing. In a few moments it was born and the ewe was up
on her feet licking the pink slime off her ungainly, large-
headed lamb. I sat on a rock to watch. Sheep and goats
normally lamb and kid in the autumn, when they are in peak
condition after the good summer grazing. But as billies and
rams run with the flock throughout the year, sometimes they
get out of kilter and there are out-of-season births. I asked the
shepherd what the lambing percentage was: from a hundred
ewes and nanny goats how many lambs and kids would he
expect to have at weaning time? 'How the hell do I know?'
he said. 'Up there in the mountains we men die, let alone
lambs.' When the ewe had licked her lamb more or less white
and half dry the shepherd tucked it into the chest pouch of
his *chola* and we walked on together; the ewe following
without bleating or making any fuss.

Just beyond Hadsar we rejoined his flock. Above the confluence of the Budil with the Gauri stream (flowing in from
the right), the flock of nine hundred was camped among the
water mills. An ancient, bent miller, his ragged *chola*, turban
and beard whitened with the dust of his trade, was impressed
by such a demonstration of wealth. 'Look at that! And it all
belongs to one family; there are so many they have to hire
men to help herd them. Here no one has a flock of more than
a hundred and twenty.'

The huge flock, with its attendant herders, was divided
into a separate camp for goats (about a third of the total) and
one for sheep. The sheep particularly looked in unusually
good condition for the time of year, with a fine wool growth.
They must have benefited from good winter grazing. They
came from a village below Karamukh, one of the hired shepherds told me, and their winter grazing was down near
Pathankot (the western extremity of Gaddi grazing). They
were on their way over to summer in Lahoul. The envied
owner – or perhaps it was one of his sons – had a bejewelled

wife and a child, who were going as far as the Kailang temple, beyond Kugti.

Most people in Hadsar are Brahmins. Many provide sweet-meat and tea stalls for pilgrims on their way up to Lake Manimahesh, at the source of the Gauri stream. Brahmins are appropriate hoteliers along a pilgrim route because food prepared by them can be eaten by everyone – even the most anxious about being polluted. Some of the Hadsar Brahmins are also the *pujaris* (priests) who officiate at the Manimahesh festival. But Hadsar was unprepossessing. Compared to the shops in the villages of the Upper Ravi, which are stocked with every commodity, the few sacks of grain and long-opened *biri*-packets in the shops here indicated a poor turnover for the shopkeepers; the villagers of the Budil valley seemed to be much poorer than those of the Ravi. It was not only the shops: people themselves looked poorer and had the manners and bearing of those who have to devote all their energy to the struggle for survival. It may be that the people of the Ravi valley, because they are nearer to Kangra, have been in a better position to benefit from the opportunity of the land market there. Many households in the Ravi valley cultivate land in Kangra as well. Or it may be that because many of those from the Ravi valley did manage to acquire additional grazing in Kangra, they have been able to expand their flocks and their profits.

We camped for the night near the flock of nine hundred, beside three water-mills. The noise of water was deafening: the Budil river roared in the distance, the Gauri just below us, and channels carrying water for the mills ran between the tents. Karma and Tchering had discovered a liquor-still in Hadsar. During the evening we emptied a bottle of the slightly yellowish spirit. The effect of the ill-matured alcohol combined with the noise of water shattering my eardrums made my head feel very odd as I made my way to bed.

From Hadsar the shepherds' migrational route continues on up the Budil valley towards Kugti. A pilgrims' route turns off the Budil valley to the right, to climb thirteen miles up into the mountains to Manimahesh.

Manimahesh lake lies at the foot of Mount Kailash, Shiva's seat. The lake is thought to be the *yoni* – symbolical genitals – of Sati, his consort; they fell here when Shiva scattered her ashes over the Himalayas. The story is that he considered he had been slighted by his father-in-law: he had not been sent a formal invitation to his *yagya* ceremony – an important gathering of all the gods. Finally Sati did persuade him to attend the ceremony, by saying, 'Of course there was no invitation. Isn't it my home?' But once they arrived there it was clear that the insult had been intended. Sati was suicidal – terrified at the thought of what Shiva might do and over-whelmed by the shame: she threw herself on to the ceremonial fire. Shiva became mad with rage, snatched her disintegrating body from the fire and performed his terrible dance of destruction, dropping bits and pieces of her body here and there over the Himalayas. That was how her *yoni* fell at Manimahesh. Lord Shiva did not lose his consort, for henceforward she was reincarnated as Parvati.

But central to the pilgrimage is a different story, the story of a local hero – Trilochen. At the beginning of the story he was a humble shepherd; then, blessed by Shiva's bounty, he became divine – in popular myth he is envisaged almost as a human form of Shiva. Possibly the association is through the name: Trilochen means 'three-eyed' and Shiva has a third, terrifying eye in the middle of his forehead.

One day Shivji, disguised as a shepherd, came to an old woman's house near Bramour and asked to borrow salt. She said she had none and that if he didn't believe her he could look for himself. He opened two chests: one was full of white salt, the other of black (for sheep). It was not that the old woman had lied but that Shivji had miraculously created the salt. 'Now,' asked Shivji, 'who will carry it up to Manimahesh, where my flock is?' She explained that her only son, Trilochen, was away at a neighbouring village and would not be home until the evening. The visitor would have to wait if he wanted to ask for help to carry it up to Manimahesh. Trilochen was unenthusiastic but felt he could not ignore expected traditions of hospitality and helpfulness. Next morning he roped the goatskin sack full of salt on to his back and they set off up the Budil valley. They had to walk twenty-two miles and climb 6500 feet. Because they carried such a heavy load they rested often, as do the pilgrims today, and many of the halts along the way are mentioned in the story.

I climbed up from Hadsar while the pilgrims were on their way down.[1] It was not a line of quietly devout people, but noisy groups of men, women and children straggling down the zig-zag path; there must have been between one and two thousand. There would be half a dozen women singing devotional songs; then, riding a pony, a fat businessman wearing a suit, or an old crone being helped along by patient sons and daughters. (How had they managed to get her up to 13,000 feet? And, having reached there, would she have been happier to die at the holy spot rather than be dragged back down?)

I wondered if a dip in the icy water of the lake had brought the pilgrims forgiveness for their sins. Were there some who were now happily confident that they, or their daughters-in-law or granddaughters, would give birth to a son? And would they acquire land, or whatever boon it was for which they had propitiated the gods? If they felt it to be so, it was not evident: I did not see anyone who looked as though they had been blessed. At the hastily built tea-shacks hungry children were gulping hot tea and sophisticated girls using bits of stick to remove mud from their smart bazaar shoes. Most of the pilgrims were not local; they were from Chamba town, or Tisa (in the west of Chamba district), or even from the Punjab and Kashmir. Youths in dark glasses, wearing slick shirts and flared trousers, and swinging transistors on their shoulders, came bounding down the hillside. They were worldly enough to assume that a European woman was fair game for ribald remarks. Perhaps they thought I would not understand Hindi. Not surprisingly they were not at all abashed when I returned their insults. They were not glowing with religious fervour nor spiritually enriched by the experience of the pilgrimage, and I became so crushed and embarrassed that I took refuge on a rock far above the path until Karma and Tchering caught up – they had not been able to resist the opportunity of another visit to Hadsar's liquor stall. The pilgrimage was clearly an enjoyable and gregarious event for the participants, but it was not as I had imagined it to be.

Many spend the night, on the way up, at Danchok. It is a bleak place, but beyond it the climb becomes even worse than the relentless pull to it up from Hadsar, and because it lies just below the treeline there is some wood for fuel. Most people take shelter in the hotel booths or sleep in the open. Few have been able to carry with them adequate bedding to ensure a comfortable sleep at 9300 feet, though in any case that would be a waste of the opportunity for convivial revelry. It was here that poor Trilochen, feeling tired and hungry, asked Shivji, 'Shepherd, where is your flock? How much farther do we have to go?'

'See,' he replied, 'here the embers of a fire are still warm, and vessels have been washed on this rock. The flock must just have moved on up.'

So they struggled up the increasingly steep path. As this reaches an escarpment it is known as the *bandar ghat* (monkey

89

bank) because you have to scale the rocks like a monkey, using hands as well as legs. I have a good head for heights and found it an enchanting place, but you must have the nerve to take your eyes off searching for a hand-hold to be able to look around. Blue poppies and *Rhododendron lepidotum* grow among the granite. There is a deep echoing roar as the river forces its way through the rocks far below.

A little further up, Trilochen and Shivji found tipped-out hookah ash which was still smouldering and knew that they were not far behind the flock. And at Barchundi, a meadow of geraniums, potentillas and gentians and a grassy knoll from which the thrusting granite cone of Mount Kailash is suddenly visible, Shiva left Trilochen, telling him to rest while he pressed on to catch up with the flock.

When Trilochen, burdened with the bag of salt, staggered up to the top of the crest and looked down on to the little lake, he could see neither flock nor shepherds, only someone's footprints. Not knowing what else to do he followed them: they led him right round the lake to the far side where there is a square slab of rock. Here he noticed ripples. Had the shepherd jumped in and been drowned? Peering down he saw, under water, a golden path. He leapt in and walked along the underwater path until he met a *sadhu* sitting beside a sacred fire. It was then that he realized that the man who had persuaded him to carry salt all the way up here was no ordinary shepherd but the god Shiva, now in meditation. Pressing the palms of his hands together in deference and fear, Trilochen asked:

'Why have you brought me here?'

'What is your trade?' demanded Shivji.

'I only know how to make the Gaddis' ceremonial *chola*.'

Then Shivji gave him enough cloth to occupy him for six months and told him he was to stay and work by the lake. (Here the story is bewildering: why was poor Trilochen made to do his tailoring at 13,000 feet ? Unless it was to demonstrate the humble tailor's devotional tenacity ; to prove that he could live and work at such a high, comfortless spot.) After he had completed the six months he was allowed home, but on one condition : that he was never to tell anyone, on pain of death, where he had been or what had happened to him. By this stage in the story he had become semi-divine, and playing the flute as he walked he followed a mythical path back home to his mother's house. There he found his family and all the village gathered for a six-months-after-death ceremony – his own. His arrival turned the wake into a welcome-home feast.

But after all these adventures his own wife was to be the cause of his death. He explained that if he gave her an account of what had happened it would be the end of him, but she chose to hear the truth. So in the privacy of their house, sadly, he regaled her with his miraculous adventures. Then he left home. And ultimately he threw himself into the river at the confluence of the Ravi and the Budil below Karamukh, where a temple to him still stands.

On their way up to Manimahesh the pilgrims should take a dip in the pool just beyond the Barchundi meadow ; it is called Gauri Kund, where Parvati used to bathe. Then on arrival at Manimahesh the *chelas* – the mediums through whom the gods speak – walk across the lake underwater. It is believed that the bottom of the lake rises up to prevent them from drowning. They surface at Trilochen's stone platform at the far side. The waiting crowd surges forward, shoving and pushing each other off the path into the water, because the man or woman who first touches the leading *chela* is the first in the queue to question the god. In the Raja's time this was his prerogative ; now it is a free-for-all. The *chelas* are usually Sipis, a low caste – as so often in this region, an essential role in the community is ensured for the less elevated. But the god's spirit can possess anyone, with such uncontrollable fervour that he or she involuntarily foretells the future.

Sacrificial goats and sheep are brought by the pilgrims; some may have been walked the week's journey from Lahoul. That evening they are slaughtered with a sickle, in the name of the god; maybe a hundred animals will be killed and eaten in an evening. The meat is cursorily cooked on whatever wood can be carried up. On the final morning, all the pilgrims take a bath. It is hard to imagine how the two or three thousand said to attend the really big festival once every twelve years can simultaneously immerse themselves in such a small lake. The echoes from the cries of *'Jai Shivji!'*, *'Jai Shankar!'* ('Victory to Shiva!', 'Victory to Shankar!') reverberate up to the glaciers and have been known to cause an avalanche.

A peculiarity of this festival is the anxiety as to whether or not you will be allowed to participate. I had been warned by people I had met on the way, 'Only those to whom the *chelas* don't object may attend. Those with whom Shivji is displeased may not come near the lake.'

On our way up, at Danchok, we had slaughtered a sheep, bought from shepherds on the other side of the river. The following night we camped beside Manimahesh. In the afternoon we had had an acrimonious argument with the *pujari* of the shrine: he claimed we were burning the wood pilgrims had left, to which as the resident *pujari* he had the right. Karma argued that we had brought it up with us; and added that, even if we had not, we were his guests at this holy place, and he should not have behaved so inhospitably or been so rude. The *pujari* shook with rage and swore at Karma. Tchering, incensed, grabbed him by the collar; Karma had to pull him off and say, all right, we would give money for the wood. Late that night when I was asleep in the tent, there was a thunderclap, so violent that the ground shuddered under me.

The storm was directly overhead. I looked out to see lightning searing vertically from above the peak of Mount Kailash down into the black water of the lake. And the tent was blasted with hailstones. I quivered: it was impossible not to feel it was Lord Shiva's wrath. Was it because we had slaughtered the sheep without invoking his name, or because of the quarrel with the *pujari*? Or was it just to make his presence felt? In half an hour the storm was over.

In the morning there was a skim of ice on the lake. Out of a clear sky the old moon was about to slip behind the shoulder of Mount Kailash. It is an awe-inspiring place. From the far end, to the south of Trilochen's platform, the full height of Mount Kailash was meticulously reflected in the water. It is a mountain that stands alone, not demeaned by any neighbouring peaks. No one, it is claimed, has climbed it. At least two of those who have attempted it have been petrified: the *pujari* had pointed out two upstanding rocks – one of which had once been a shepherd, the other a sadhu. Semi-naked figures stood on the rocks off the far shore, cupping the holy water over themselves and invoking Shivji. Though they were only a hundred yards from where I stood, they looked very small, dwarfed by the scale of the mountain. At the shrine, which bristled with tridents and was gaudy with new red flags, an offering was being made and the bell rang out in the silence to alert the gods. In the far distance, down at the grazing ground, a shepherd called to his flock.

It was a memorable experience to be somewhere so magnificent and also so frightening. It was disturbing to feel close to a power quite indifferent to mankind, and to know that for thousands of years men have made their way here to propitiate a deity whom they believe to be an embodiment of that power. Yet in spite of those centuries of pilgrimage, the place was unscathed by man. Man-made efforts – the shrine, the path round the lake, and the odd plastic shoe or paper bag left by the pilgrims – seemed insignificant. Here the landscape is as it was when the Himalayas were created, and will never change. I felt small and vulnerable, and felt my previous lack of faith was improvident : I was ready to respect the gods.

The Upper Budil valley from Hadsar to Kugti – which at 8000 feet is the last village on the northern arm of the V of Gadderan – is wild and pretty. We were back on the shepherds' migrational route, following the path as it skirted rock faces on projecting platforms. Elegant deodars – providing shade of unrivalled quality – reached up towards the sky, their web of roots gripping perpendicular rocks. It was difficult to believe that Raja Sahil Varma and his army of Gaddi mercenaries must have come along this path on their way to conquer Lahoul and Kulu. Though the wayside shrines bore offerings of fresh flowers, there were few travellers except for shepherds and their flocks. On the opposite bank there was the white zig-zag line of a flock picking its way in single file across the cliffs. The Budil river flows fast through the narrow valley ; it is not quite a gorge, but in places it thunders far below the path.

Down there I could just hear the forest contractor's labourers struggling with a jam of timber. The fifteen-foot sleepers, of deodar and spruce, become entangled like a pile of spillikins. There is no way to transport them down the valley except by river. The labourers (unhappy Kashmiris and Garhwalis brought in by contractors) shouted at each other against the roar of the river, as they leapt from sleeper to sleeper. Wielding iron rods they tried to prise away the sleepers that lay on top or on the edge of the tangle.

Once or twice we met Public Works Department labourers desultorily working on the path with a pick or shovel. They were Gaddis – old men and young girls who had been sent out in order to add the meagre wage paid by the Public Works Department to the family income ; while the more able-bodied tended to the important work in the fields or with flocks.

The path descended through deciduous woods and emerged at a substantially built bridge across the Budil. It was blocked by sheep and goats; shepherds were taking the opportunity to count their flock, making sure there were no stragglers. But suddenly there were cries of anguish. One of the shepherds was gesticulating wildly at the far end of the bridge. Another, throwing off his heavy shoes, ran down the bank towards us. It took me a moment to understand. Then I saw a ewe struggling in the water; she must have been pushed off the bridge. For a second or two at a time you could see her head, then she was submerged, tumbled by the muddy, snow-melted water of the fast-flowing river. The shepherd on our side plunged off the edge of a gravel bank into the river as she swirled towards him, somehow grabbed a leg and heaved her on to the gravel. She lay there; I thought dead. But he picked her up by the hind legs and gave her a jolt and she came to life and staggered back to join the others on the bridge.

Just before Kugti the river bed widened into level, green banks and shallow, stony beaches. As I walked towards them I could see huge brass vessels bubbling on several different hearths and groups of turbaned men sitting on the rocks. I thought it might be a picnic or a cremation, but it was a flock being clipped. A flock-owner does not clip his own sheep alone: he depends on neighbours and other shepherds, who are paid for their help in wool. First the sheep must be washed. A small stream, not too fast-flowing or dangerous, is dammed. Then shepherds try to force the sheep to walk through it to the far bank. They are reluctant to plunge in, and many have to be caught and mercilessly thrown into the water by the increasingly short-tempered shepherds. (Goats are not clipped; only the extra-long hair, just above the belly line, is cut. The hair is too coarse to be woven for anything but bridles, mats, snowshoes and waterproof over-capes.)

The shearers sat on the ground, in a line. They held the sheep upright against their bodies and clipped slowly, carefully and close to the skin. At home in Scotland it would be considered too close to the skin, dangerous for sheep soon to spend cold nights at 14,000 feet. The close clip is because they want wool with a good length of staple; but it has had only a few months to grow since the winter clip, and the sheep have been in poor condition. At this time of the year the yield averages a mere two to three hundred grams per sheep. In the autumn, because the sheep have put on condition during the summer, the staple is a little longer and the yield nearer half a kilo.

It was a social occasion. No one was in a hurry – there was certainly not the atmosphere of a sheep-shearing competition. There was time to stop and talk, and take long, slow drags on the hookah.

It is the flock-owner's duty to provide food and drink for his helpers. The meat and rice were cooking in the brass vessels; and as the sun began to set, women came from the village carrying basketfuls of fried chapattis and many bottles of *arak*. I knew the riverside party went on well into the night because I heard the revellers making their way home long after I was in my sleeping bag.

Kugti had none of Bramour's atmosphere of an ancient, holy place. It was a sprawling village of undistinguished stone and timber houses. There was no shortage of timber – every trough was a hollowed-out tree trunk and the courtyards were enclosed by barricades of unhewn wood. The village had an aura of timelessness: the school was a dusty yard, where only occasionally lessons were taught; there was one tea shop, no shops. The villagers belonged to a remote 'interior'; they were not like the outgoing villagers of the Ravi valley. They talked of the winters, when they are isolated by thirty feet of snow. I felt it to be a place introverted by its isolation; where today's event soon becomes a legend, and there is no way of telling whether the origin of the story was something that happened the previous year or hundreds of years before.

The cattle had bushy tails and upright, spreading horns; they had yak blood in their parentage. Yaks can stand cold, high altitudes and poor fodder better than ordinary cattle. To introduce new blood – for the hybrid cross begins to deteriorate by the third or fourth generation – yak bulls have to be brought over the Kugti pass from Lahoul. A hornless bull can cost three thousand rupees – they are highly valued as draught animals in Lahoul, for there someone leads the beast while another drives the plough. But here, as the draught bullock is not led, they can import cheaper, horned bulls. Recently the *pradhan* of Kugti and the government vet went to Lahoul to buy new breeding stock. With the money collected by the villagers they succeeded in buying two young yaks at a good price – 1900 rupees. They had managed to manoeuvre the beasts over the 16,000-foot Kugti pass and were heading back down to the village, when – so they said – one of the two lost its footing on the glacier and rolled into a crevasse. The disappointed villagers may have doubted the story – they climbed all the way up to the glacier to look for the bull, though alive or dead they could hardly have hoped to get it out. They could not see a sign of it in any of the crevasses, nor even of its disappearing tracks.

I had known about the tragedy soon after it had happened. I had happened to hear it in Lahoul, from a Gaddi who had come over the Kugti (alone, as he traded illegally in musk-deer pouches). Now, two years later, the story had become a village legend. So many sheep had disappeared from the grazing ground below the pass that Kugti people believed the lost yak had become a *bhut* (a ghost) which haunted the area. I asked an old man whether he thought the story of the yak's fall into the crevasse was untrue and, if he did, what he thought had really happened. . . .

'Who knows? These days it is probably working for a rich Lahouli. How do we know that they ever bought two yaks? Just drank half the money while they were there, maybe, or bought themselves *charas* to smoke or to sell. In the old days we could trust each other. Nowadays, who knows what's happening? We thought there was something wrong with their story when they told us. Then later we knew they had told lies because the *Devta* punished the *pradhan*: his son fell into the river and was killed – they never found his body.'

On one of the days we were in Kugti there was a festival. All afternoon and early evening groups of three or four men swayed up and down the village. They held hands and hauled each other here and there; the marigold garlands round their caps becoming increasingly bedraggled. It was like 'first footing' at Hogmanay: groups of people staggered from house to house carrying a bottle of the local spirit. Later in the evening, when the day's work was done – the fodder gathered, cattle brought home and the food cooked – the girls and women came out. Arms linked, they made their way up the narrow, muddy paths between the houses, singing. Then at the far end of the village, on a round paved yard, they began to dance. Braziers of resinous wood fitfully lit the darkness, and the flames gave a ghoulish look to the glowing faces. A young, sober boy played the flute; an older, much less sober, man drummed an erratic beat. The girls danced in a wide circle, preferring the rhythm of their own singing to the drum beat. Two or three men would stagger into the circle and, much to everyone else's amusement, wave their arms and bodies in a semblance of dance, but they soon shuffled away to sink again against a supporting wall.

We were standing in the shadows watching when we were suddenly dragged away by a young man in a smart new-looking *chola*. He had heard that I was the one who stayed at Deori. He explained, a little incoherently, that he was Sat Pal's daughter-in-law's brother. He pulled me up a ladder made of a hewn-out tree trunk into a small, crowded room, lit by a piece of flaming wood balanced on a wooden chest. I was made to sit on the felted goat-hair mat in the place of honour beside the host and was plied with platefuls of gristly dried meat and brass beakerfuls of brown *arak*. I made some attempts at polite conversation but the party was past the conversational stage. Our host sank into oblivion, his head buried in the pleats of his neighbour's cloak. Soon I scrambled out into the black night and cautiously felt my way between the house walls and down slippery stone steps. Snatches of song rose above the river's roar as a returning reveller made his way home along the far bank. I could trace his lurching, irregular course by the orange light from his flaming torch.

As we left Kugti and set off on the first day's climb towards the pass, we met a *pujari* from the Kailang temple – two miles beyond the village. Climbing up the steep path he told me the story of Kailang Nag (snake), the old god of the temple, and of how a long time ago he came here from Lahoul.

'He came because the people prayed and prayed for the disease that was killing all their cattle and sheep to stop. He heard their prayers. He came from over the pass. He was a snake and he was brought over by a ram, twisted round its horns; he stopped at Dugli. It is a place two miles above where the temple is now. After he arrived the disease stopped. Sixty or seventy years later he moved to a spring near Darm. Now, that was a place very high up, very cold and difficult for people to get to. So they weren't pleased. They begged his *chela* to ask the *Devta* to move again, to come and live somewhere further down, nearer the village. Soon the *chela* had the answer: the people were to throw a *bhana* [a cymbal] as far as they could, and where it hit the ground they were to build a new temple. While they were digging the foundations for the temple, at the spot where the *bhana* had landed, they discovered in the ground a stone image with three heads. It was very difficult to get it out, but when they did heave it clear a stream of clean water began. Ever since then this has been the most important temple in the valley – people come from far away to have the *darshan* of Kailang Nag. Yes, the image is stone with three heads. Many people offer a goat or sheep and shepherds kill a sheep in his name to protect their flocks.'

I had read that, much later, Raja Siri Singh presented an image to the temple, cast in the auspicious eight metals – *ashtadhatu*. This image is of Kartik Swami, son of Shiva and Parvati, god of war. He is said to be an upright figure holding a spear; his head is covered with snakes and his waistband and sacred thread are also snakes. I imagine it was presented after one of the Raja's successful military expeditions over to Lahoul and Kulu. But I was not to see it.

As we approached the temple steps I noticed that fresh blood had dripped on them, and a large vessel of water was boiling on a hearth within the temple precincts. Then I saw, at the top of the steps, sitting at their ease in the dark shade of the outer platform, the owner of the nine-hundred-head flock and his bejewelled wife and child. They explained: the wife and child, a son of two and a half, had travelled all the way here to perform the son's haircutting ceremony at this auspicious temple. A boy's first haircut has a similar significance to that of a Western christening. The *chela* shaves his head with a pair of sheep shears, an offering of money and a goat are given, and in return the deity assumes responsibility for the child's welfare. The *pujari*, with whom I had walked

100

up, was so in awe of the importance of the occasion that he refused to open the inner shrine, lest I should pollute it, or upset the god's concentration on the proceedings. He told me to come back next morning, which was impossible. So I had to carry on without the benefit of Kailang Nag's *darshan*. In spite of the rebuff, as I sat on the platform looking down the Budil valley and out towards the pristine mountains, I somehow felt that at that moment the gods were well disposed towards me. The little boy played marbles with the walnuts he had received as *prasad*, and I prayed for a safe crossing of the Kugti pass.

1. A detour, described out of context – in fact, the pilgrimage is usually at the end of August or in early September.

CHAPTER FIVE

Blue Grass and Arak

*Over the high passes
to summer in Lahoul*

Just beyond the Kailang temple there was a shrine beside the path, noticeable from a distance because it was so crammed with tridents and iron rods. But unless it had been pointed out to me, I would not have noticed that there was also a flag-bedecked trident on the opposite side of the river, away up on the top of the cliff. It would be unwise to ignore these, for they are shrines to the *devi*. Here she is Mirkula of Udaipur;[1] on the Lahoul side she is more often referred to as Baghpatti. Whatever her iconography she is the *Devi* of the Kugti pass. Whether it is possible to cross it, and what hazards have to be faced on the way, depend on her mood and her opinion of you. Shepherds may take a new piece of red cloth or an iron trident to offer at the shrine on the summit. They will certainly make an offering of food; if possible, it should be bread made with fat and sugar. And, most important, they will take care not to try her patience or to give her an excuse to be in a bad mood.

During the three days' climb up from Kugti, what we heard made us begin to appreciate her significance. On the last night before crossing, we were camped below the pass at about

13,500 feet, when well into the night I heard a large flock pass by. In the morning, as we were packing up, an anxious shepherd came bounding back down the hill. Had we seen four pairs of pannier bags full of rice, eight kilos of it? We had not. The shepherds had made careful plans: because there was no grass at the top camp, they had kept the flock grazing lower down and had taken the animals up after it was dark. So when the panniers, full of the precious rice, had slipped off, they had not noticed.

'Ah well, that'll teach us, we should have had more trust in the *Devi*; then she would have provided for us and the flock. Now by searching for it we have got late and the rocks will be falling at the black patch.'

That morning I had no forebodings about the *Devi*'s mood. I still had the feeling that the gods were with me. It had been such an idyllic walk up from Kugti to the top of the Budil *nala* that I was heady with a sense of well-being. We had woken just before dawn to a pale cloudless sky; for hours before that flocks had been streaming past our camp.

Before crossing the high passes, over this spur of the main Himalayan range, shepherds must wait until the snow has melted enough to be able to cross in a single day; in an average year that will be towards the end of June. As a result, the grazing on the approaches to the passes becomes over-crowded. We had seen dozens of flocks on the alps above the tree-line, in a lovely glen where the stream coming down from the Kugti joins the Budil. The day chosen for a flock to cross depends on the decision of the oldest and most experienced shepherd in the group. To try to avoid the overcrowded grazing, some shepherds may take their flocks off to a side *nala*. Others, impatient to be among the first over, and on to the new growth on the Lahoul side, may risk a fodderless night camped on snow. But their newly clipped and thin animals have little resistance to the cold, particularly on empty stomachs: they may succumb to colds and coughs and even pneumonia. There is also the chance that once over the pass some of the animals may be too weak for the tiring struggle of coming down through the snow, which softens as the sun rises. One of the reasons for our own pre-dawn start was the shepherds' anxiety to get down while the snow was still reasonably firm.

The night before we were to cross, Karma and Tchering had sat up making stuffed *parathas*, cooked on the remains of the wood we had carried up the hill. I had gone to sleep lulled by the rhythm of the dough being slapped between the palms of their hands. Tea in bed was before dawn, the *parathas* were wrapped to be eaten later, camp was quickly packed, and we were off well before sunrise. The snow was hard and the walking, over what later in the summer would be loose moraine and boulders, was easy. But it was deceptive; every twenty paces I had to pause for an extra breath. I had begun to feel the effect of the thin air and the need for a steady rhythm – I realized I was counting one-two-three-four as I climbed and stopping for an extra breath every twelfth step. The path was well trodden by thousands of sheep- and goat-hoofs. I could see it way ahead, zig-zagging up the clean snow, and could hear the shepherds shouting at their animals.

There was a thousand-foot glacier to struggle up, still covered by a carpet of snow; though tiring, it was not dangerous. But, in September, when the flocks are on their way back south, the snow cover may have melted and then crevasses are dangerous. A glacier is like tissue paper under pressure: when the tension becomes too great, often on a curve, a crack appears – gradually or suddenly with a sinister creaking – creating a narrow green chasm. The greatest danger is when there is a thin cover of snow, disguising the chasm but too thin to support you. The shepherds, and indeed the goats and sheep themselves, pick the safest route. You might be following what is clearly (by the dung and hoof-prints) the main track, when, if your eye is quick enough, and it has to be, you may notice a small trail of fresh hoof-prints turning off the main track. You must follow it, or (as once happened to me) you face an impassable crevasse five hundred feet down, and, tired and angry, have to climb all the way back up. (It was in one of the crevasses here that the yak was claimed to have been lost.)

Above the glacier it was much steeper; a thousand feet up a narrow gully on loose rock, shale and icy snow. A line of goats and sheep was straggling up. We waited, worried that they might dislodge bits of rock. Sheep and goats often break each other's legs when a stone, dislodged by one of the animals above, comes bouncing back down a steep hill. Shepherds are expert splint-makers; winding pieces of cloth round neat lengths of stick, tight enough not to slip down a wounded leg, yet not so tight as to stop the blood flow.

The last two hundred and fifty feet to the 16,000-foot summit were unpleasant. Now I was gasping for breath after every five steps and the wind was better. Karma kindly gave me his company; Tchering was up way ahead, though we could not see him. For the Kugti summit is not actually a pass (a *jot*), but is known as the Kugti *galu*. Passes are open saddles; a *galu* is a neck, and that is exactly what the Kugti is – a neck between the rocks. Its shrine was unassuming – a few bells, a scatter of tridents, red prayer-cloths being battered by the wind and a slab of rock for the offerings: five boiled sweets still wrapped in cellophane, the corner of a fried chapatti, a lump of *gur*, two four-anna pieces and a fifty-paisa coin. We had been warned that whatever you have with you must be fairly shared between all the companions and the *Devi*. We shared out a little of our stuffed *paratha* but, though I wanted to have time to take in the view and to enjoy the achievement of being here, the sun was by now high in the sky and we had to move on; we knew it was the north, the Lahouli side of the pass, that everyone dreaded. So snatching a look back at the wild beauty of the peaks of Shivbhumi and a last glimpse of Mount Kailash, we set off.

Below the *galu* there was a steep traverse. Halfway down it was the dreaded 'black patch'. It is here that the *Devi* is most likely to air her bad mood, or demonstrate her disapproval of those who have failed to respect her. Here she takes her merciless toll on any party which attempts to cross the pass lacking in 'straightforward courage and a tranquil spirit'. When Lahoulis cross the Kugti on their pilgrimage to Mani-mahesh, they are reluctant to have a woman in the party. '*Dil shant aur sidhe hone chahiye,*' they say – the heart (or spirit) must be peaceful and straightforward or the *Devi* won't let the party cross. It is not clear whether women are thought to have intrinsically tremulous hearts, or whether the presence of a woman in the party causes others to waver. Also the *Devi* does not like noise: there must be no shouting or hullabaloo – a precaution in itself against the danger of starting a land-slide or an avalanche.

The 'black patch' was a wide stretch of black shale. The danger was immediately evident; those who suffer from vertiginous tendencies would not want to stop and look. The path was only wide enough to put one foot in front of the other. We had to stop because once again the way was blocked by a flock, waiting to cross the hazardous stretch in single file. That morning I was feeling so full of self-confidence that I dug my stick into the semi-frozen shale and, resting some of my weight on it, looked up. Standing up against the skyline, a thousand feet above, was a crest of loose stones and rocks. The instability of the Himalayas was obvious: I could see the tracks made by stones which had fallen out and others which at any moment might break loose. That is why the pass must be crossed before the sun is too high, while the night's frost still grips the stones on the crest. Hurtling down from a thousand feet above, it would not have to be a large stone to hurt you, and here you would not have to be hurt much to be killed: looking down from my precarious foothold I saw there was a fifteen-hundred-foot perpendicular drop to the glacier below. Then, just in front of me, a ewe butted a well-grown lamb. For a second he tottered, but failed to regain his footing and over he went, slowly at first and then faster. The shepherds did nothing: there was no point. I understood why shepherds, and all who must cross the Kugti (and there are other passes with similar reputations) are in such awe of the *Devi*. And I was relieved to feel myself to be in her good books.

We wanted to get down far enough to camp below the snow, but ahead there were still some nasty traverses. My confidence began to ebb – it needed such an effort of concentration to make sure that every foothold was a sensible one. This was no place for snow-sliding. By the time we reached the long moraine it was well after one o'clock: the snow had begun to get soft, and it was tiring to walk through. Stragglers from the flocks were sinking down in the snow, unwilling to move on. The shepherds, themselves exhausted and exasperated, heaved them on to their feet and kicked or pushed them on down the slope.

We managed to struggle to the foot of the moraine and camped well below the snow, at 12,000 feet, on a wide flat ground near an extraordinary temple. I have not seen one like it anywhere else in the West Himalayas. A large upstanding rock is encircled by a platform of stone slabs; the shrine itself is on the side facing the pass. The temple is to Kuldeo (the god of your tribe, caste or family); here it is Lord Shiva. The rock bristled with tridents. Placed on the shrine there was a curious collection of objects, as though someone might have set them out for a 'Kim's Game': a number of bells, one handsomely embossed with the image of a god; a large, very white conch shell; a ladle for burning juniper, which is used as incense; a flat bowl with a stand at the end of its handle so that it could be set down horizontally; a brass holder for a *ghi* lamp; a cheap brass plaque of the goddess Lakshmi; and some heavy iron double chains attached to rings – these are used by *chelas* for self-flagellation.

The *pujari* of the temple was a Gaddi who had the grazing 'run' on the escarpment just above. Perhaps the income from being *pujari* helped to offset the poor grazing. Here, on the main migrational route between the Budil valley and West Lahoul, you did not need a trained shepherd's eye to notice the devastated pasture. The slopes were criss-crossed, every two or three feet, with a herring-bone pattern of paths made by sheep and goats. Thousands of destructive hoofs had dug into the soil as the flocks ate the herbage and its roots; so that gradually the soil had begun to slip away from the criss-crosses.

To be the *pujari* of this temple is not an insignificant position, for it is an important place of sacrifice – like the Kailang temple on the Kugti side. He described proudly the annual occasion when the shepherds who have 'runs' in this *nala* sacrifice ten or twenty goats to feast the villagers. Not, he was anxious to point out, as a part of dues which have to be paid to the Lahoulis, but out of their bounty. He enthused over the quantity of blood and thought I would be impressed by his descriptions of copious food and drink.

The sacrifice I witnessed was not on such a lavish scale. Camped here, we met again the shepherds whose ewe had fallen into the swirling waters of the Budil. In gratitude for her successful rescue they had promised a sacrifice to Kuldeo. There was an older man, Jagdish Ram – small and spare, without an extra ounce of flesh, he had a bony, aquiline nose and a handsome handlebar moustache – and two young men, Ram and Kapur Singh – the former Jagdish's son, the latter his nephew. The animal to be sacrificed was a small male goat. Ram Singh sharpened a brass-handled sickle, while Kapur made the offering out of dough; he moulded it into the shape of a flour bag with an elongated corner, and fried it in *ghi*. They filled the ladle with burning, smoky juniper. Jagdish and his son then went to the shrine. There they presented the burning juniper and the fried flour-bag bread, tied a new red cloth to one of the tridents and rang the bell. Meanwhile Kapur took the goat once round the temple and at the far side sprinkled water over its back with a juniper twig. If at this moment the sacrificial animal shudders, it means the god has accepted it. It did, and amid cries of '*Jai Shiva! Jai Shakti!*' its head was cut off; Ram Singh was holding it while Kapur dealt the blow with the sickle. They held the pulsating, truncated neck over a brass vessel to collect the blood, which was carried once round the temple. To the eerie echo of the conch shell being blown like a trumpet (the trumpeter turning to face all four corners of the universe), the steaming blood was offered at the shrine and painted on the three spikes of a trident. Then they began to cook the meat, later to be enjoyed by us all.

Just beyond the temple, the path climbed up two hundred feet to some cairns, before going on down to cross a lower moraine. This was our first view of Lahoul itself; from the pass, only the distant 20,000-foot peaks had been visible. The contrast between this terrain and the monsoon-watered country we had been walking through was dramatic. The main Himalayan range (or the most eastern spur of the Pir Pinjal) is a barrier to the progress of the monsoon. The Kugti pass crosses this range; so do the Rothang and the Hampta to the south-east, and the Chobia and the Kalicho to the north-west. All these passes are regularly used by shepherds and their flocks. Forests, lush growth and humidity were left behind. Here there was a vast sunlit landscape. The air was dry and aromatic with juniper and artemisia. It was inhospitable terrain: frightening glaciers, the sudden cannon-shot sound of an avalanche, crests and pinnacles of rock and crumbling earth – precarious after centuries of frost and eroding wind. Landslides and rock faces scarred the treeless mountainsides. I could just make out a finely drawn line which ran horizontally across the mountain towards the inverted fan-like shape of an old moraine. Then, suddenly, there was a green patchwork – which was fields – and some brush strokes of paler green – which were willow groves; and clustered on one side were substantial, flat-roofed houses. That horizontal line running two or three miles across rock faces and round escarpments was an irrigation channel. In Lahoul the rainfall is so scanty (an annual 23 inches of precipitation, which includes the winter's snow) that without irrigation no crop can be grown, not even the willows. The vivid green patchwork was made up of irrigated crops of barley, some wheat, a root called *kuth* (*Saussurea costus* – Lahoul's original cash crop) and many fields of potatoes.

But for the arriving shepherds, for men like Jagdish Ram (and Sunni Devi's husband, who of course may be thinking only about *arak*) coming down from the high passes, it is not the carefully irrigated potato-fields that are interesting. Nor is it the fragrance from the pink banks of *Rosa webbiana*, nor the prayer flags fluttering from the Buddhist *gompas*; but the growth of the *niru*, the blue grass, and the *mat* and *morar* grass. Jagdish and his son and nephew come from a village near Baijnath in Kangra. They had left their winter grazing grounds early in April and had been on the move for nearly three months. They had had a convivial fortnight near their relatives' village in Gadderan, and there the flock had had a rest from daily marches. But by the time they arrived here, they were tired of the anxiety of being on the move and their animals, particularly the sheep, which are less good scavengers along the way, were in poor condition. And the last stretch over the high passes is testing for an already weakened flock.

Jagdish and I sat up at the cairns and he looked keenly at the hillsides on the other side of the main valley. His summer 'run' was up the Miyar *nala* – a side valley coming into the main valley further downstream. The grass varies considerably from year to year, depending on the quantity of winter snow and spring rain. In a good year, to the expert eye, the pastures should have a blue-green tinge below the snow-line. This blue grass is never luxuriant but it is extraordinarily nutritious. There must be a special ingredient in the soil to grow such fine potatoes and such rich grass. And for the shepherds the aridity, if it is not excessive (when the grass does not grow, or soon burns dry), is an advantage. Flocks do not thrive on the rank, misty slopes of the monsoon-saturated hills: they suffer foot-rot and laminitis.

So Lahoul's grazing runs are sought after. From the cairns, gazing over the sweep of mountains, I found it hard to believe that all the grazing runs on every stretch of the vast hills belonged to particular flock-owners.[2] Gaddis and other migratory shepherds, too, notably Kuluis, have moved up here for the summer for hundreds of years. J. B. Lyall's interest in the Gaddis brought him, in the early 1870s, all the way from Kangra to see for himself the famous Lahouli pastures. It was he who first made an official note: 'A short fine grass of a dull blueish-green colour called *niru* is the flocks' favourite food.' He discovered inconsistencies in the grazing rights: that Gaddis paid different rates from Kuluis, that dues for some grazing were being paid to the *thakur* (feudal overlord), others to the villagers themselves, and that some 'runs' were not being used. So he had all the possible runs listed. 'I took a great deal of trouble in collecting these rights in Lahoul sheep runs and think that the entries may, with considerable confidence, be presumed to be correct.'[3] He issued permits for the runs to many Gaddis from Kangra. It may be thanks to Lyall that today so many Kangra-based Gaddis summer in Lahoul (though there are those from Gadderan, too), and as a result have larger than average flocks.

We, and all the flocks coming down from the Kugti, easily crossed the Chandrabhaga by a substantial bridge. Today the main river and most of the side *nalas* are bridged. But it was not so in Lyall's day. He said that the one here was in such bad repair that shepherds often lost sheep while crossing it. And championing the Gaddis, as he so often did, he commented that if the Lahouli villagers enforced their right to a sheep for every flock that crossed their *jhula* bridge (a basket-box on a pulley), then in return the *jhulas* should be kept in good working order.

Most shepherds stopped at the first village for a glass of tea at the 'hotel', some for a bottle of *arak*. Also they had to buy rations; while on the move, especially coming over the high passes, they cannot carry much with them. We stopped, too, and while we waited for a kettleful of *chang* (local beer) and bowls of hot meat dumplings, I watched negotiations over the price of a goat. At this time of the year shepherds are less likely to want to sell sheep. Goats' weight remains comparatively steady, while that of sheep varies according to their condition. It is more profitable to sell sheep in the autumn, when they are fat after the summer's grass. The price of meat in Lahoul is always high, because Lahoulis are keen meat-eaters and have the cash to spend on it, and because, at this time of the year, after the long winter, they have no stock of their own. A kilo of meat cost 50 rupees, whereas the top price in Manali or Kangra might have been 25.

But the shepherds did not dawdle near the villages: their

hungry flocks were not welcome round the cultivation. In Lahoul, to have fodder to last the cattle and flocks through the long winter, hay banks must be irrigated and guarded against intruding cows and sheep. Most Lahouli villages and fields are at 9000–11,000 feet. Crops can be snowed on before they have been harvested in September and they may not be free from snow for ploughing until May. It is a very long winter, and the fact that animals have to be housed indoors and fed limits the amount of stock that can be kept. Traditionally Lahoulis have been traders – or monks or nuns – rather than owners of large cattle-herds or flocks. In summer the small domestic flocks are taken out to graze each day. Boys and girls (or the village simpleton) take them up on to the steep, sometimes crumbling hillsides above the village; often the house cows and the few sheep are herded together. They are always brought home at night. The yaks, draft *dzos* (a yak–cow cross) and yeld cattle are sent up, usually unattended, to the higher pastures further afield. And, as they largely keep to the valley floor, and as cattle and flocks graze differently, the grazings (*dhars*; or *thangs* as they are called in the Tibetan languages) above 11,500 or 12,000 feet are available for the migratory flocks.

We arrived at the head of Miyar *nala* with Jagdish's flock. It is one of those rare open areas occasionally found in the higher reaches of a Himalayan valley; unexpected while following the precipitous path along the narrow gorge lower down. I watched the flock reach its 'run'. The hungry sheep fanned out, heads down, running from one juicy tuft of new grass to the next. The weakest animals lacked the strength to benefit from the *niru* shoots or the primulas. Too exhausted to move, they sank down near the summer dwelling – a stone shelter built against an overhanging rock. The shepherds loosened their packs, tossed out the kids and lambs they had been carrying in the chest pouches of their cloaks, and crouched down to peer into their home. Was the precious firewood they had hidden away last September still there? Or had the villagers or other shepherds taken it? At this height there is little fuel; only juniper scrub, its smoke stings the eyes, or yak- or goat-dung. Then they leaned back against their blanket packs and lit a hookah. Jagdish sighed – 'We've arrived, thanks to the gods. There's not much grass yet higher up, but it'll come on.' For two months there would be less day-to-day anxiety and plenty of time.

During July and August I spent some time here at their camp at Thanpattan, at 12,500 feet. Twenty flocks have 'runs' in this area; some are from Kangra, some from Gadderan. If there are four or five men with a flock, one of them may go home once it is safely arrived at the summer pasture, to attend to the cultivation until he is needed for the autumn migration. Or sometimes there is a changeover; one brother goes home, and another comes up here in his place. The year before, Kapur Singh's cousin had been here with the flocks while Kapur Singh went home to attend to the maize fields. The latter was not pleased that this year he was to spend the summer up here. Ram Singh plodded on, not caring how the gods or his father chose that he should spend his days. But Kapur was less fatalistic: he hankered after the bazaars and liked to talk. While we were there he spent a lot of time with Karma and Tchering.

At the beginning of the summer the flock used the lower part of the 'run', allowing growth on the higher slopes, more recently clear of snow. Flocks of sheep and goats are seldom grazed together. A familiar morning noise was the sound of two of the shepherds calling to the sheep and goats as they moved off in opposite directions, while the third shouted and pelted stones at a recalcitrant beast that had a mind of its own.

Two or three weeks later they moved their base up 2000 feet higher. Then the goats were separated from the sheep for days at a time; Kapur and Ram had to camp up with the goats, while old Jagdish stayed with the sheep. Sheep are seldom grazed above 14,000 feet, but goats are happy at 15,000 or 17,000 feet. Surprisingly, they feel the cold less and, adventurous and surefooted, are more adept at feeding on precipitous rock faces. At the end of the season, when the lower slopes had some re-growth after their mid-summer rest, they moved down again.

But the grazing pattern varies with the lie of the 'run'. If it covers two different *nalas*, first one may be grazed and then the other, rather than the lower, then the upper slopes. And if the quality of the pasture varies between two or three adjacent runs, the groups of shepherds have a long-established arrangement of rotation. Every second or third year each flock will have the use of the particularly good or bad pasture. There is remarkably little confusion and there are few arguments about the animals. Sheep and goats are sometimes marked by nicks cut out of the ears; especially necessary in a flock with several different owners. Occasionally I have seen a couple of stragglers being led back to their own flock. But the shepherd's eye is so familiar with each beast that an intruder, or an animal that has gone missing, is quickly noticed.

Old men like Jagdish Ram, veterans of decades of summers in Lahoul, become well known in the locality. The shepherds have regular contact with villagers. They go down to drink *arak* or *chang*, and to buy small quantities of tobacco, wheat flour and *sattu* (parched barley flour) from them. Where fuel is so scarce, *sattu* is a useful fuel-saving cereal, as it can be stirred into milk, curds or water without any cooking. Rice is more economical on fuel than chapattis (of either flour or maize), but it is expensive here and not easily available;

though shepherds try to keep a small stock of it, as they are particularly fond of rice boiled in goat's milk.

Over many generations the visiting shepherds have each established connections with one particular household in the village below their 'run'. Unless there has been an unusual rift, it is expected that that household will continue to supply some day-to-day rations, act as their mail box and often as their pub. Shepherds seldom buy liquor as a 'carry out'; if they did, it would be finished before they reached camp. They use going down to see if there are any letters, or the need for two or three kilos of *sattu*, as an excuse for an afternoon's drinking; it often becomes an all-night affair.

Soon after the shepherds' arrival at Thanpattan, Kapur Singh had gone down for some *sattu* as their flour was finished. He was expected back that evening. It became dark and it was raining and cold – he still had not returned. I had eaten and was dry in my tent. We only had a handful of flour left and some tea to offer. Jagdish and Ram Singh, inside their dripping igloo, were hunched on their hunkers beside a smoky goat-dung fire; they had milk, but that was all. Hungry, they spent the night wrapped in their double-weight and doubly shrunk blankets (these are very waterproof, though once wet they take for ever to dry). At about ten next morning, when the wet blankets laid over the rocks were steaming in the sun and the sheep and goats were huddled round the igloo – neither Jagdish nor his son was willing to take them out to graze until they themselves had had something to eat – Kapur Singh appeared. He was obviously suffering from the night before: he made no apology, nor were there any recriminations. He simply took the goatskin sack of flour off his back and sank down for a smoke.

Keeping the summer camps stocked with basic rations needs forethought. Those who bring their own ponies (which means they must cross by the Rothang or possibly the Hampta pass, as none of the others is muleable) send them down to the bazaars to return laden with rice, *gur*, wheat flour, a little dal and salt – for themselves and also essential for the flock. Those who do not have their own ponies and who are at remote camps on the Lingti plain or in Spiti order from merchants in Manali, or Keylong, while on their way up in June. The transport has to be arranged with a muleteer; usually belonging to a family who has handled their trade for generations. Sometimes the transporter is paid in cash, sometimes in kind – usually in wool. Jagdish Ram shared a mule-train delivery from Udaipur, the bazaar town in the main valley, with neighbouring shepherds. The arrangements usually involve several groups of shepherds together, as muleteers operate caravans of ten or a dozen animals. Such co-operative transactions are unusual in an area where few trust anyone outside their own family (or even within it).

One morning I met two Lahoulis, tramping up the valley carrying heavy coils of wire rope.

'Where are you going? What's that for?' I asked.

'It's the Gaddis. We're to make a *jhula* across the river away up above Thanpattan. Shepherds from below Bramour want to go back by crossing into the Sauch *nala* and then over the Cheni pass. So they arranged to have the wire brought and we're to make a *jhula*. It'll only take us a couple of days and we're being paid a big ram. My father is a muleteer – he's been dealing with these Gaddis for years, bringing their rations up for them.'

The equipment to build the *jhula* would have cost thousands of rupees and the sharing of the expense between different groups of shepherds must have required considerable organization. Moreover, the concept of building a bridge, rather than accepting that from this side of the valley it was impossible to reach the pass over to Sauch as there was no way across the river, revealed unusual enterprise. Increasingly, I began to appreciate that Gaddis are far from being simpleton sheep-herders.

Most Lahouli households brew their own *chang* from barley, using a special yeast, and distil *arak*, also from barley. Both *chang* and *arak* can be very good; the latter needs to be well matured, and the best is flavoured with juniper. *Chang* is sold by the kettleful; *arak* by the bottle. Usually shepherds who come for a drink sit in the kitchen–living room, like visiting neighbours and the family itself. Shepherds passing through villages where they are not known, though, would expect to be treated more like customers in a pub. Then they will ask for a bottle and sit in a separate group; helping themselves from it – and from another and another.

I was visiting a family in Kanjar, the top village in Miyar *nala*, when shepherds called in for a drink. I had seen them around Thanpattan; they were camped at a run a little above ours and they were well known in the village. They joined the circle where we sat cross-legged on carpets and goat-hair mats, facing in towards the stove. The iron stove, standing on a clay mount in the middle of the room (it had a chimney straight up through the ceiling) is very much the hearth, the hub of every household. We were all served by the wife and daughter of the house. Though the shepherds later paid for what they had drunk (or a rough estimate of what they had drunk), they were treated as guests and with the ritual formality guests deserve. In front of every two or three people was a low, narrow stool for the drinking bowls. No one took a sip just when he felt like it, only when the wife or daughter came round with the bottle and kettle and, bending down, gesticulated – 'Drink up, drink it dry.' Then she refilled the

cup to the brim, but it should not be touched until she came
on her next round. Often she chided one of the shepherds –
'Come on, come on, you're not going back to your flock in
the wilds tonight. You'll eat your food here.' Gradually, the
evening that had begun with discussions on crops, prices for
potatoes and wool, and general gossip, turned into a ceilidh.
There were snatches of Gaddi songs:

> O Gaddi, go from home
> O Gaddi, go by Kugti pass
> O Gaddi, go with bare feet
> O Gaddi, go with bad luck
> O Gaddi, go awake, awake
> O Gaddi, go down Jobrang *nala.*
>
> O Gaddi, go to your camp
> O Gaddi, go, having left your children,
> O Gaddi, go to Miyar *nala*
> O Gaddi, go by motor
> O Gaddi, go smelling of *arak.*

And the family and neighbours sang local Lahouli songs, as
well as tunes from Bombay movies that everyone knew from
the radio. The women of the house, while they did the cooking
and served the drinks, joined or, rather, led the singing, and
many of them joined in the drinking, too. Even the toddlers
of three and four were given a few sips of *chang.* Dishes of
boiled potatoes and chutney were put on the benches as
cocktail snacks, and later on bowls of broth were served. But
by then the shepherds had begun to slump against the walls;
their drags on the hookah (smoked through the clenched palm
so as not to touch the mouthpiece) and its bubbling became
less intense, and slowly they became silent and expressionless. When shepherds go for a drink it is not a question of a
social drink or two, but a desire to be drunk: a thirst for
oblivion to escape the monotony of every day.

*

For an outsider like me to observe the details of the shepherds' summer days was a pleasure. For me, Thanpattan was a place of tranquil beauty. In the evenings I would stand up on the ruins of the *gompa* and look down on the river meandering through the wide valley, cutting its path through the green turf studded with gentians, potentillas and anemones. It was a very different landscape from the contrasting greens of the wooded valleys to the south. Here there were hills and mounds like sand dunes, and small lakes, marooned after the river's meanderings, glinted darkly in the evening sun. As it sank lower in the sky its rays gave sharp definition to the glacier – to projections and buttresses that seemed like a mad giant's construction, and to scars and cracks where the ice was slowly shifting with an almost perceptible movement. Sometimes there was the intermittent sound of a flute, carried down valley by the wind – a shepherd waiting for his grazing flock. It was a romantic place: it had that timeless, grand beauty that gives you a twinge of pain at the bottom of your chest, as though your rib cage were too tight.

But try to envisage what everyday summer life is like for the shepherds. For us it requires an effort of will and imagination, a conscious determination, for it is so unlike any day-to-day life one has ever experienced. It is monotonous, and there are hours and hours with nothing to do. Kapur Singh said: 'When you're on the way, crossing the pass, looking for grazing, you don't think; you do what you have to do. You want to arrive here, to rest. But what sort of life is this? Here there is nothing. There are no medicines when we are ill. I have this watch [most of the shepherds wear a watch], but there is no radio, no bazaar.'

I asked if he visited the video parlour in Udaipur. 'How often can I get away to go there? Once, maybe, I get the chance.'

For those who must live here for sixty or seventy days, each day is too much like the last. Soon after dawn, they were up and out (they sleep inside the igloo or out of doors, depending on the weather and the temperature) for a smoke in the early sun. Kapur Singh milked a goat for tea and for the morning meal. They never use sheep's milk; they say the ewes do not have enough and the lambs would suffer, but it seems that they simply do not like the idea, and they believe that goat's milk keeps them healthy. Ram Singh would light the fire with some dry juniper twigs and then put the yak's dung to burn up while he made the dough for chapattis. Old Jagdish eased himself up from his smoke to spread salt for the flock and fetched water from the spring two hundred yards away. By then the tea had brewed. Ram began the task of slapping the thick chapattis between his palms before firing them on the *tawa*. All this took two or three hours. By ten the morning meal, chapattis and milk, was ready. Once it was eaten and the dogs fed (with the same food, on their separate iron *thalis*), the brass vessels were burnished with ash and put to dry on the igloo roof. It was time for another fill of the hookah.

Finally the lambs and kids which were too young to go out for the day were caught and put in a stone pen, covered with a check blanket. Then there was the familiar cacophony of sheep being separated from goats, as the two younger men set off in their opposite directions. Kapur had a flute tucked into his *dora* and each of them had a *chilam* and tobacco pouch in the chest of his cloak. It could take an hour to cajole their flocks as far as the day's appointed grazing. There they had to spend four or five hours. They would sit on a rock, or lie back against a bank while keeping half an eye on the flock, half just staring out at the opposite hillside. Or they would while away some time playing the flute, or snooze some more.

Meanwhile Jagdish would set off with a rope to gather a load of juniper, or to scrounge for yak dung. Or he stayed at home. He put the dishes of medicinal herbs out to dry, and stretched out the goatskin that was being cured for use as a sack, or he might churn the goat's milk, *lassi*, to make *ghi*. If there was a goat or sheep recently killed by a fall or a falling stone, or if one had died from a non-putrefying disease, he put the meat out to dry in the sun, cut into small pieces. No shepherd will kill one of his own flock, and even if he has sold one for slaughter he will not allow it to be killed any-where near his camp: presumably a traditional taboo in case hunger or greed leads shepherds to decimate their own flocks. Some days Jagdish spent much of the time meticulously stitching a goatskin tobacco pouch or sharpening his sickle on a stone. Or he, too, slept away the rest of the day.

Sometimes he would be lucky and a visitor from a neigh-bouring camp would stroll up for a chat and a smoke. The previous summer shepherds at Thanpattan were worried about marauding dogs that had once or twice worried the flocks. 'No, no, these aren't shepherds' dogs. Our dogs are all right; otherwise we would beat the life out of them. I don't know where they've come from; they've gone wild.' I asked if they gave names to their dogs (though they treat them well, they do not show them much affection). 'Of course. How would a dog know who he was if he didn't have a name? We give names to our sheep and goats, too.'

If two or three visitors arrived, or if the two flocks were grazing near enough for Kapur and Ram Singh to keep an eye on them from the camp, they passed time playing a complicated game called *koda*. It used two 'boards'. A large flat stone was marked out like a chessboard, criss-crossed with lines scratched on it with a stone, and set out with some pebbles – this was a scoreboard. The game itself was played on the ground, or on a blanket, using cowrie shells. I never mastered *koda*. But we had packs of cards and spent long afternoons, in the burning sun, playing rummy. Sometimes Kapur, who was the brighter of the two cousins, would be bold enough to

challenge Karma or Tchering to a game of *sip*. But only occasionally did he have the luck to take money from them: more
often he was the one who had to delve into his leather pouch.
Sip requires fast mental arithmetic, and their card-sharping,
bazaar skills were usually too much for him. Jagdish and Ram
never ventured beyond rummy.

At five or six o'clock the flocks straggled back into camp,
bleating for their lambs and kids, and soon settled themselves,
huddling close into the igloo, for the night. Bears and wolves
can attack the flock, and so the dogs, which are kept as guards
rather than as herders, were protected with spiked iron collars.
The evening meal prepared and eaten, the three men shared
a hookah almost in silence and by the time it was dark, soon
after eight, they had buried themselves in their blankets for
the long night ahead.

Occasionally there was a letter from the home village. I
asked the men if they worried about their families at home.
'What can we do out here? What's the good of worrying?
Often we don't know anything until what was happening has
happened.' I met three men coming down the valley who
showed me a well-thumbed telegram and asked me to tell
them what it said. It was in English, and not easy to interpret.
'Ram Lal son of Goshan Lal left home 25th your arrival
expected.' Did it mean that Ram Lal had left home to come
up here? they asked. It did not say so. Or was it, as I suspected,
and as I think they did, too, gently announcing that he had
left home for another world? The telegram had reached them
the day before; it had taken six days to find them. They went
on down the path, with the prospect of a four-day journey
home before they could find out what had happened.

Perhaps those back home worry more: mothers, sisters and
wives who know only too well the dangers of daily life on the
mountainside. Once I had seen shepherds carrying a body on
a makeshift stretcher. It was their companion, who had been

killed when a stone, dislodged by one of his own flock, flew down out of the slope and hit him on the head. They had had to carry the body down to below the treeline to find wood for the cremation. I was impressed by their stoicism and over-awed by the scene of the six mourners alone in the indifferent mountains. There had been no wailing or signs of emotion: they were dealing with the consequences of an act of the gods.

The older men have become inured to this life. The younger ones are more restless. Kapur Singh hankered after wearing a shirt and trousers and sauntering in a bazaar. There must be romances with Lahouli girls; I passed some shepherds sharing salty butter tea with a group of giggling girls out for the day to repair a *chorten* (Buddhist memorial cairn) and imagined that from such incidents romance might spring. I was told that today it happens less than it used to, because the Lahoulis are more self-conscious now about their own status and therefore more apprehensive of casual encounters. But an enigmatic old song, describing such a romance, is still sung with feeling. Its story runs that there was a Lahouli girl whose family disapproved of her love of a Gaddi boy. During the winter some Lahoulis met the boy, Bonku, in Kangra and purposely deceived him, telling him that Bhotli had died. He was so grief-stricken, he killed himself. Two summers after-wards the shepherds told Bhotli how her sweetheart had died; then she killed herself, too:

> 'I met the Lahoulis, oh Bhotli
> How are you? What is the news of you?'
> Listening to the news of Bhotli
> Three times he hit himself in the chest
> Because she had died, because she had died,
> Three times he hit himself on the pass.
>
> 'I met the shepherds, oh Bonku
> Two summers have gone by,
> How are you? What is the news of you?'

Listening to the news of Bonku
Three times she hit herself in the chest
Because he had died, because he had died
Three times she hit herself on the pass
She, too, died after that,
So said the Gaddis, so said the Gaddis.

At home in Gadderan or Kangra, women like Sunni Devi may worry about their menfolk, or complain at the thought of them drinking too much Lahouli *arak*, but they accept their absence and the anxiety with resignation. They would not want their men to give up shepherding, because of the cash income – from the wool and from the sale of surplus stock. But one afternoon a young man like Kapur Singh may lie back against the bank and decide that next year he will not be a shepherd. He may vow to himself that he will emigrate in the opposite direction from that taken by his ancestors four hundred years ago; that he will travel back down to the plains, search for a cousin who he knows is living in Pannipat, outside Delhi, and chance his luck at finding a job in a tea shop or a grain store.

1. Or Mindhali, of Mindhal in Pangi.
2. Himachal Pradesh Forest Department says that 140,000 head of sheep and goats pass through Manali every spring. A few of these summer in the Kului side valleys above Manali, and some go over into Spiti, but the Manali figure does not take into account the flocks coming into Lahoul over the Kugti, the Chobia or the Kalicho passes. The total figure for Lahoul is probably well over 100,000. Dues are paid to the Forest Department once a year: 40 paise per sheep, 60 paise per goat. Forest guards make checks to see that the fee has been paid. In addition to these official taxes, a token payment is still sometimes made to local villagers or to the *thakur* or his descendants, often in kind – two young rams or a breeding goat. I once met a relation of the *Thakur* of Gemur striding up the barren Baralacha at 15,000 feet to make sure he collected his annual rent.
3. From J. B. Lyall, *Settlement Report*.

CHAPTER SIX

The Devi Thwarts Our Plans

so it's down the road through Kulu.
Autumn

The monsoon comes in from the south-east. By the end of August, at its most north-westerly extremity, its strength is waning. The clouds penetrate into the mountains less frequently: it is misty and wet for hours rather than days at a time. The air currents are changing. On the high tops the warm rain no longer melts the snow, and the snow-line stops receding; instead there is a fresh dusting of whiteness. Early in the morning and in the evening there is a crispness in the air. Autumn is beginning and September and October are among the loveliest months.

It is time for the shepherds and flocks to leave Lahoul and head back towards the valleys on the south-west side of the main range. They usually cross before the end of the month of Bhadon (during the last week of August or the first ten days of September – the Hindu months, being lunar, move against ours). If it has been a year when there was little snow in Lahoul, so that the grass never grew properly, or a year when lack of rain meant it quickly became burnt by the sun, then the shepherds are forced to make an early start back towards the post-monsoon grazing. Even if the grass in Lahoul has been good, they do not want to linger too late for fear of early snow blocking the high passes. Often they are more ready to make long-term weather predictions than to forecast the immediate future. If you ask 'Do you think it will turn to rain before nightfall?' you are likely to get the answer 'Who knows?' But you often hear them ruminating over the long-term possibilities. 'It'll not rain until after the full moon of next month.' Or 'There'll be snow before the potatoes are out of the ground.' The source of the rumour may have been an old man pontificating after a kettle or two of *chang*, or it may have been the oracle of Jamlu, the presiding god of Lahoul, at a formal consultation. Or perhaps in these mountains immediate, local conditions are difficult to predict, but the old shepherds do acquire an instinctive knowledge of general weather patterns.

Flocks which have spent the monsoon in central Lahoul, up at the source of the Bhaga river or in its side valleys, or away beyond the Baralacha pass, begin to move down to cross the Rothang pass into Kulu. Others, who have been in eastern Lahoul, round the headwaters of the Chandra river, or on the Spiti border, may cross into Kulu over the Hampta pass. Jagdish and his flock, with the graziers from Miyar *nala* and other side valleys of the Chandrabhaga, cross by the higher passes further to the north-west – the Kugti, the Chobia and the Kalicho.

Jagdish decided to leave towards the end of August. As I had to delay my departure for a day or two, we planned to meet him the far side of the Kugti pass, at the top of the Budil *nala*, where the flock would stay for a few days' grazing.

By the time we set off towards the Kugti it was early September. In the morning, as we left the last village, it began to rain. I was emotionally ill at ease and had upset morale within our party. As we struggled up the dreary, grey moraine in the cold rain, I remembered the warning about the necessity for a 'peaceful heart' and I knew mine was not. Nor was any of us as 'tranquil' as we ought to have been if we were to cross the pass in safety. I began to dread the wrath of the *Devi*, the 'black patch' and other unknown, unimaginable and fearful dangers. But at midday, when we were camped in the wide arena around the open-air temple to Kuldeo, the rain stopped and the clouds began to disintegrate and roll away. Above us the last of the summer flocks were climbing on up to camp below the pass (the villagers had told us that Gaddis had left before dawn that morning). We were at 12,000 feet; there was fresh snow lying an inch thick 1500 feet above us, but there was still a day before we had to cross the pass, and the next day's sun would surely melt it. Later the sunny afternoon turned into a brilliantly starry evening; so clear you could see every star in the firmament. I stood out in the sparkling black and white night; I felt ashamed of my lack of courage and smiled at my fears and imaginings of the morning. The weather was set fair, and unworried I went back to my tent.

The instant I was wakened by banging on the fly sheet I knew what it was: snow. There had been no moon; now there was an eerie light and that special quietness that comes with snow. Karma was knocking the snow off the tent and calling out, 'The kitchen tent has already collapsed and the others need clearing!' It was two in the morning. There were a good three inches of snow lying and it was still blizzarding.

By dawn the snow was five inches deep. As early as 6 September – and we were only at an altitude of 12,000 feet. Half an hour later the shepherds and flocks who had gone up came down. They were cold and wet and indignantly astonished.

'The sky was fine and clear in the evening – how did it happen? Now we'll have to go down and round by the Rothang pass. It's a long way round. It's not our route, but what's the point of trying to cross from here? Up there the snow will take a week to clear; more likely it won't clear at all. It's not worth the risk of waiting.'

I cringed and crept away. I knew they had been caught in the rage that the *Devi* had directed at me.

We, too, had to turn back down and go round by the Rothang pass. If I were to cross the Kugti again I would need to feel I had adequately atoned for angering the *Devi*; for lack of self-confidence itself can be dangerous on the high passes. And I would ensure that first I had propitiated her generously.

Maybe I over-dramatized. But years spent in the Himalayas do not inure you to their dangers: on the contrary, you become increasingly respectful of them and of the power of their deities. Why else would the shepherds themselves have turned back that morning? And if I was so affected, it must be much more fearful for those who have been brought up to believe in the wrath of the gods, and who must daily risk themselves and their valuable flocks on these dangerous mountainsides.

So we retreated forlornly back down the Jobrang *nala*, and for three days had to follow the motor road up the Chandra valley towards the Rothang pass. By now the hillsides were a faded brown and yellow that merged with the grey of the rock slides and shale slips. The sweeps of mountain were colourless: the only colour was in the great rock faces, in the strata of igneous rock in the granite – white, ochre and red. But high up on the hillsides there were green, irregular circles. Not fairy circles; the green is the rank growth round a summer camp, where generations of sheep and goats have eaten every edible grass and flower and fertilized the inedible nettles and docks. On the far side of the river, flocks were crossing a sheer rock face in single file, a thread of small white dots moving at an inconsistent pace. The roofs of the square village houses were no longer flat: turrets of stacked hay gave them a fortified look. The barley and wheat had been reaped and the potatoes were being dug. (The valuable seed potatoes, vital to the Lahoulis' economy, must be transported over the Rothang before snow closes it for the winter.)

By conventional standards the motor road was insubstantial. For long stretches there was no metalled surface. Often it forded side streams not by a bridge or culvert but by plunging into the river. In places the berm of the road had been eaten away, eroded by wind and snow; though it was only when I had gone round a corner that I realized that the edge of the road had been five hundred feet up in mid-air. The last village on the road out of Lahoul is Koksar. It is a line of scruffy tea shops: the resting stop for buses, trucks and flocks before the grinding ascent to the pass. Beyond Koksar the road takes mile-long zig-zags backwards and forwards across the bare hill, but mules and flocks go straight up.

For the flocks the Rothang is as much of a thoroughfare as the Kugti and the hillside is just as criss-crossed with tracks made by their sharp hoofs. Dozens of flocks cross in a single day. But it was not only the baa-ing and bleating of sheep and goats and the grunting calls and whistles of the shepherds that disturbed the silence of the mountains. For shepherds who have spent the last two months in the quiet of some secluded valley, the shindy on the Rothang must be like arriving at Old Delhi railway station. Muleteers swore at their beasts. Trucks ground up the hill at ten miles an hour; their noisy diesel engines spewing out fumes. Buses careered round the hairpin bends; each driver hoping to blast everyone out of his way by holding his hand firmly on the horn – though men and animals paid little heed.

The summit of the Rothang is at only 13,200 feet, but I found the climb up the north side gruelling. It may have been my despondency, or because from a short way above Koksar I could see how far it was to the top; the full horrors of most passes are hidden until you are relatively close. I was angrily gasping for breath – Karma and Tchering, imagining the delights of Manali bazaar, were away ahead – when I heard a holler from below. It was a muleteer friend and his empty mule train on their way back from delivering rations to a Lahouli village. I was soon in the saddle or, rather, *on* the high wooden saddle, which was covered in Tibetan carpets, and, soothed by the lead pony's bell, I suddenly found the ascent of the Rothang a pleasure. I could exchange pleasantries with co-travellers, appreciate the stark beauty of holy Mount Geyphang jutting up into the sky, and see on the left, to the north-east, the incredible spread of the mountains of Spiti – beyond them lies Tibet.

For hundreds of years the path across the Rothang has been an important trade route. The British spent considerable resources improving the track for caravans carrying Indian goods north and returning from Tibet and Ladakh with borax, rhubarb and the famous *pashmina* (cashmere) wool. The wool trade was valuable and the British were anxious to divert some of it towards British India, rather than see it all disappear to Kashmir. But though for centuries a main trading route, and not really high, the Rothang has always been treated with respect. There is a dangerous and sudden wind; from time to time people crossing it, particularly the slow and poorly clothed, still die. There is no shelter, and a clear sunny morning can quickly turn into a bitter blizzarding noon.

There is a story explaining the origin of the mortal wind. When people first lived in Lahoul there was no pass: Lahoulis had no way out of their mountain fastness. From the wind and the birds they heard that to the south there was a wonderful country where the grass was always green and there were thick forests. Some went to search for a way out, but none returned: all perished in the snow. The people despaired and braced themselves once more to accept the long winters and short growing season. But, some years later, they were possessed again by a desire to see the green valley. So they sacrificed a virgin and appealed to Lord Shiva to turn his attention to their predicament. Shivji, the easily enraged, was furious that they had not come to him earlier, and demanded another virgin before he would consider the problem. Then he appeared. Still in a rage he hurled his *trishul* (trident). The mountains swayed, the sun disappeared and the birds were silent. When daylight returned the Lahoulis saw a pass. Two thousand feet down, on the Kulu side, there is a huge, upstanding cone of granite: this is Shiva's *trishul*, petrified; after cutting its way through the pass it landed here. To make sure that people would always be reminded of their lack of faith in him, Lord Shiva cursed the Rothang with a wind – icy and dangerously sudden. That is why even today's travellers should treat the crossing with respect.

But the day we were crossing the weather remained sparkling clear, though the wind was cold, and the Buddhist prayer flags, suspended from rock to rock on the left of the summit, were fluttering and spreading their prayers. None of us wanted to loiter. Sitting on my pony I was cold, so I took to my feet. A mile or two down the footpath I could see into Kulu. For the shepherds who have spent months on the barren Lahouli hillsides, where every combustible twig is so precious, the forested slopes ahead must arouse anticipation of companionable fires. The air is soft and gentle. Hillsides are covered with dark green deodar and fir forests, crops grow with little effort, and the orchards of plums, cherries, apricots, pears and apples produce abundant fruit.

Kulu looks attractively green and wooded, but the migratory flocks find it increasingly inhospitable. In comparison with neighbouring valleys – even others which do receive the benefit of the monsoon – it looks like a history-book illustration of England after the eighteenth-century land enclosures. British settlers acquired land to plant orchards –

much of it had been 'marginal', uncultivated land. More recently, Lahoulis, with the proceeds from their successful *kuth* and potato crops, have bought land. Most of that, too, was previously uncultivated land that had been used for grazing. And orchards have become so profitable that the Kuluis themselves have enclosed all available spare land and planted apples. So many a grassy knoll or shady riverside willow grove, where shepherds used to camp, is now a carefully guarded orchard. Then the Forest Department is energetic in its replanting and re-forestation; timber grows particularly well here – Kulu's deodar forests are famous. So areas where flocks grazed within forest land are now fenced off as 'reserved forests' or nurseries for young trees. A great number of sheep and goats have to come up and down the Kulu valley. The shepherds moan, 'All the way, right from the top of the Solang *nala* to the very end of the valley at Aut, there's nowhere good to graze, or even to spend the night.'

In September the flocks are in good condition, at their peak after the summer grazing. Once over the Rothang, so that there is no chance of snow locking them on the wrong side of the main range, they are not in a hurry to move down towards the congested valley floor. There is a brief period of conviviality. Many migrational routes from the summer pastures converge in order to cross the pass, so the shepherds meet relations and friends whom they have not seen for some time, and will not see again for many months.

Two thousand feet below the Rothang, just above the treeline, is Murhi, a hamlet of 'hotels', and a halting place for all buses, trucks, tourists, mule trains and flocks. The shepherds settled their flocks to rest in a sheltered glen and, abandoning one unfortunate man who was to look after them, set off for a 'hotel'. I watched a group make themselves at home in the dimly lit interior of the canvas-roofed shack. With their homespun tweeds, bare legs and stout leather shoes they looked different from the other customers – like the noisy group of Bengali tourists well wrapped in hats, scarves, gloves and galoshes. The shepherds stared in amazement, but were not diverted from their bottles of livid-pink 'country' liquor and plates of meat, *kurhi* and rice.

An argument began with the hotel owner over the price of a large ram. She was a Khampa, very much a business woman, with a forthright manner. She teased the shepherds as she served them:

'Yet another plate of rice? Do you men not know how to cook? You've eaten nothing over there in Lahoul all summer? What? Pay you eight hundred rupees when I can get a leg, bigger than there'll be on this one, for eighty rupees from Manali bazaar and get it brought up on the bus? If I buy this, we'll have all the butchering work to do ourselves. Has Lahoul made you greedy as well as hungry? Take it away down to Manali and see what the butcheress with two husbands will give you for it.'

The Gaddis gave as good as they got:

'You think I'll offer one like this to her? I'll take it down to Bilaspur where they've never even seen a sheep this fat.'

Ultimately the sale was settled, with the hotelier paying 725 rupees and giving the shepherds their food (but not their drink) 'on the house'.

I was told that not long ago, at this time of the year, a flock was camped on a relatively gentle slope below Murhi, just within the tree line – among the lovely silvery birches. The slope is above a spectacular rock face. At night, despite the guard dogs, a bear got among the flock. Perhaps the shepherds had had too much pink liquor to be woken either by the dogs barking or the goats bleating – sheep are silent when frightened. Although normally herbivores, when bears wake up hungry in the spring they do sometimes eat carrion, and then can develop a taste for meat and attack young lambs, or the old and weak animals. The flock panicked and all three hundred hurled themselves over the rock face. The mess of the carcasses at the bottom was so terrible that neither meat nor wool could be salvaged. The scale of the shepherds' tragedy was appalling. They had known every animal since its birth; daily they had protected them all from natural and unnatural hazards; now they were dead and the capital they represented gone – shepherds have no insurance. One would have thought that a disaster on this scale might turn them against shepherding for ever. But it was not so: I was told that, later, the shepherds involved in the accident had been given two hundred animals. I did not think to ask who the contributors had been. It would have been interesting to know whether they were relations or neighbours, and what the terms of the gift had been – such generosity towards another's loss is not common.

From Murhi we came scampering down the old mule route. The motor road contours away from it, taking loops through a newly replanted and fenced forest, to where it joins the old mule and sheep track at Kothi. One year I came from Manali to attend a Gaddi dog show there. I had come up in the jeep, and offered local people a trip up to the show. 'A dog show? What's that? Will there be swings and ferris wheels and sweet stalls?' The idea of dogs being exhibited to win prizes was incomprehensible to them. At the turning to the Kothi rest house there was a colourful banner across the road: 'GADDI KUTTA SHOW'. *Kutta* (dog) is not a polite word in Hindi, and the sign caused much amusement.

The show had been organized by the Indo-German Farm Forestry Project from Palampur, Kangra. The project leader had been so impressed by Gaddi dogs – their broad chests, sweeping quarters, wide heads, strong jaws and long black-and-tan coats – that he had become interested in them as a breed. He was about to export a pair to Germany. A dignitary from the German Kennel Club had travelled specially from Munich to see the breed in its natural setting, and there was also a German couple from Kathmandu, from the Kennel Club of Nepal. It was bad luck that it was a late year. Because of heavy snowfalls in February and March, and continuous spring rain, the snowline had not yet receded as far as Murhi; the flocks were still down in the side valleys. As we parked the jeep beside two Mercedes we could not see any sign of sheep, goats, shepherds or dogs. The judges and their supporters were gathered on the rest-house lawn. There was a Gaddi among them, but he had come in one of the Mercedes to help look after the prizes – two merino ram lambs.

By midday the only entry was our own four-month-old puppy. The judges had inspected her teeth and admired her tan eyebrows and muzzle, shiny black coat and 'well set' tail. A little later, with a lot of giggles, some village boys dragged a scraggy yellow mongrel from behind the rest house. The judges were not amused. The organizers should have realized that because of the unusually late snow shepherds and flocks would not yet be in the vicinity. Perhaps the international travel arrangements of the visiting VIPs had made it impossible to postpone the show. Or perhaps it had been thought that prizes of merino rams would be enough of an incentive for shepherds to make a special journey with their dogs; even if they had to abandon their flocks. But it was not so. At one o'clock the event was cancelled. To our great disappointment, we were not presented with one of the prizes, though we were the sole entry. Rather than the two rams having to be transported back to Kangra in the Mercedes, they were left in the charge of the rest-house *chaukidar*; some shepherds had been asked to pick them up when they passed this way. The

opposite: The Kugti pass, at 16,000 feet. The flock, below the crest of the pass, are crossing the dangerous 'black patch'. *overleaf:* Sheep following shepherd down from the pass; a track can be seen on the right where one has slipped.

above: A goat resting on a shepherd's summer dwelling, Miyar *nala,*
while *below:* Jagdish sits inside it making chapattis.

left: A shrine at the Kuldeo temple, Lahoul; it consists of ibex horns,
tridents, iron chains and cloth.
overleaf: Summer camp. Kapur Singh is churning *lassi* in a goatskin sack
to make *ghi.*

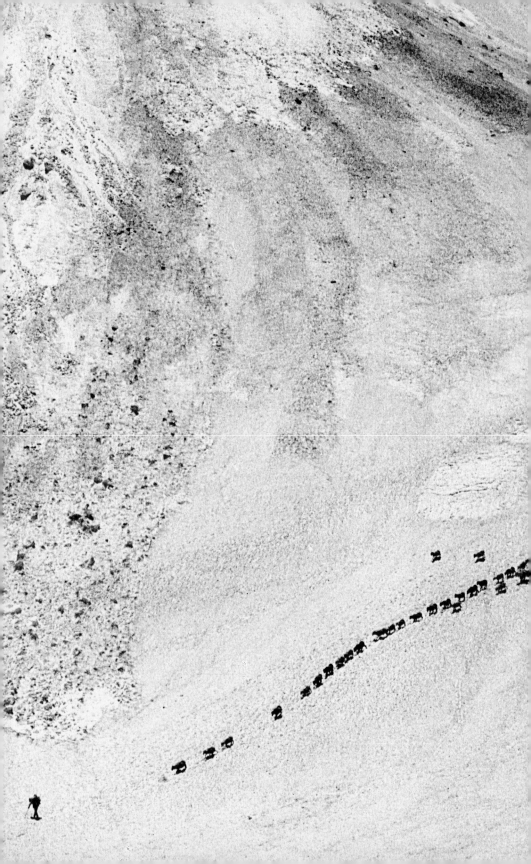

chaukidar was not impressed by the fact that they were carefully bred merinos. He told me (well out of earshot of the dignitaries) that if tourists staying at the rest house wanted a meat feast he would not hesitate to sell the sheep.

The aim of the 'Indo-German Integrated Farm Forestry Project, Dhaula Dhar' is to relieve the pressure on natural resources, 'to stabilize the man–land relationship'. As part of the work towards that overall aim, in 1980 the project invited an economist, Hans Herbert Bormann, to 'assess the conditions of shepherding among Gaddis'. His report was to suggest specific undertakings to help gain a better control over shepherding, to reduce the number of animals, to reduce the proportion of goats to sheep, to increase the benefits to be derived from shepherding and to suggest alternative employment for shepherds.

Bormann worked with the support of the Himachal Pradesh Department of Agriculture. His report is the only official study on the Gaddi shepherds and their problems, and the problems they are said to create. He collected many useful statistics and came to many sensible conclusions. But, perhaps owing to his short stay in the area – a brief visit to the winter grazings and three months in the project area – it seems to me that he misinterpreted some of the issues. As he saw it, Gaddis had little cultural identity apart from their attachment to a geographical homeland. He considered that the association of the Gaddis with shepherding was only made by outsiders, on the strength of their distinctive 'shepherding' clothes; and that this identity was not important to the Gaddis' idea of themselves. The comments he heard from Gaddis themselves – their complaints about the difficulties of a shepherd's life and the unenthusiastic attitude of the younger men – seemed to support his view.[1] This encouraged him to assume that if they were

opposite: A Gaddi, carrying his pack and blankets, a child across his back and a young lamb in his chest pouch.

offered good incentives, many would throw away the shepherd's crook and become bee-keepers, angora-rabbit farmers, Public Works Department labourers or herb-gatherers. It did not occur to him that there was little chance a shepherd would admit that he was doing well. To ask a shepherd details of the profits and losses of his flock is a little like asking someone to reveal their bank balance. And a shepherd giving an optimistic answer would be tempting fate, or the gods. I am sure there are shepherds who could be enticed away from flock-owning, but there is a good chance that they would be those least receptive to learning a new husbandry: the brightest and most efficient are doing well enough not to want to change. (I would guess that twenty years hence the frustrated, intelligent Kapur Singh will be resigned to a life of shepherding, and doing very well.)

Bormann included two suggestions which would amuse the shepherds if they heard them. He, too, was an admirer of their dogs but thought it was a shame that they were not trained to herd the flocks. He suggested the owners should be given instruction on how to train them to perform like German shepherd dogs. I can only suppose he had never experienced running a dog round a flock above a Himalayan rock face.

Another idea was to introduce South American llamas; his theory was that migratory flocks were undesirable in the winter pastures, which he would rather see ultimately closed altogether. The summer pastures in Lahoul would therefore become empty, too. To these he suggested importing wild llamas, though he did not mention where they would go in the winter. The shepherds who were out of work, he thought, could herd the llamas and, additionally, 'the domesticated llama could be tried as a pack animal. This animal could even prove useful to shepherds if they would try to improve their very spartan way of life.' I had a picture of a frustrated shepherd trying to persuade a stubborn, spitting llama along a precipitous path – too narrow for the llama's baggage. The shepherd would have had to offload the accoutrements of his new non-spartan life, like tents and sleeping bags and camp furniture. . . .

Below Kothi rest house, scene of the dog snow, we crossed the Beas as it roared into an eerie gorge and thundered through dramatic cliffs. We had been striding out, anxious to reach Manali that night. But I stopped at a sad sight (though it might have encouraged Bormann). An old shepherd and his two companions were sitting at the side of the road, disgruntled. The old man was at the end of his tether. Since he was here last autumn, the bank he had envisaged as his midday halt had been turned into a potato field. His flock were cheerless, too, lying on the road, panting in the midday sun, trying in vain to protect themselves by clustering into the short shadow from an overhanging rock. A car came hurtling down the road, full of Indian tourists who had been up to play in the snow. As it screeched to a stop inches away from the sheep, the youngest of the shepherds rose slowly and indignantly. The tourists shouted: 'What the hell are your sheep doing on the road? We'll have them all kebabed for dinner. You're certainly good for nothing but *charani*. Baby *ulu*, can't you see in the day time?' (*Charani* – a herder – is abusive in Hindi, as is *ulu* – an owl.)

After the gorge both the river and the road turn left into the main valley and run gently down the five or six miles to Manali. The narrow terraces were yellow and deep red with ripening maize and millet. Behind us new snow shone on the Solang range that blocks the head of the valley; Shukerbeh and Murkerbeh rise to 20,000 feet, and on the far side of them are the Budil *nala* and Kugti. I hoped Jagdish and his flock had not waited too long; I imagined they realized that snow

147

had prevented us joining them. A flock or two had found a halting place on the alder islands in the middle of the clear, aquamarine Beas river.

It was not only Karma and Tchering and I who were looking forward to the pleasures of Manali. No other town the shepherds pass through matches its excitement. It is hardly a town, more of a shanty-town bazaar, but by comparison Bramour is a sleepy village. Keylong may be Lahoul's district headquarters, but the bazaar is hardly worth the name; Kulu has a government hospital and district courts and a dull bazaar; and Mandi, Baijnath and Palampur are conventional small towns with shops for cloth, shoes and kitchen utensils, chemists' and radio- and watch-repairers. But nowhere can match Manali's many glass-plated restaurants or the dozen video parlours, or the shawl shops, or the Tibetan-run fancy bazaar – with foreign goods smuggled in from Nepal or bought off the hippies – the shops selling frozen chickens, the beer bar, the 'English wine' shop and the dual carriageway. Shepherds sit on the kerb watching the entertainment. During the last fifteen years Manali has grown into a popular resort for tourists from all over India. There is also a varied and colourful population of European 'travellers'. No wonder the shepherds stare.

It is a prosperous place: there is plenty of money about. Partly it is from tourism – from hotels, guesthouses, restaurants and shops – and partly from the thriving apple and plum orchards and the potatoes.

When I was first in Manali, in 1970, there was only one butcher and the next one down the valley was in Kulu. Now there are twelve butchers in Manali alone. In 1970 a kilo of meat (all cuts are sold at the same price) cost five rupees; now it is twenty-five rupees. Goat's mutton is more often available than sheep's, as the shepherds are loath to sell sheep except in the autumn, when they are at their peak weight. (In September the mutton from sheep fattened on Lahoul's grass is some of the tastiest I have ever eaten.) Manali's new demand for meat is not unique: there has been an increase in meat-eating throughout the Punjab and Himachal and it has had an accelerating effect on the shepherds' income. Few people in these areas are vegetarians: meat is thought to be good for your health and it also enhances your status. As more and more people have the money to buy it, the price continues to rise.

In Manali there is also a thriving wool industry. It has been based on the manufacture and sale of shawls; Kulu shawls are renowned throughout India. Recently sweaters, scarves, gloves, socks and tweed have become popular. Some of the raw wool comes in from Lahoul where, as sheep are clipped only once a year, the wool is long-stapled. Yet more sought after is the Biangi wool, after many years beginning to re-appear on the market, brought down by mule caravans from Ladakh and Tibet. Some raw wool is bought directly from the Gaddis, but it is not highly esteemed, being short-stapled and coarse. Some is bought from the Gaddis by agents, taken down to the plains to be manufactured and spun in the big mills in the Punjab, and brought back up here to be re-sold by different agents. And some weavers in Manali use wool imported from Australia and manufactured in the Punjab. Like the meat trade the wool market is growing, if not quite so fast. Not so long ago in Calcutta and Delhi, and Himachal, too, when the chill evenings of winter began, a fine old shawl would be brought out of a trunk year after year. Now fashionable girls like to have a colour-coordinated shawl for every costume.

Bormann's view that many shepherds are willing to give up shepherding is further undermined, as I see it, by the fact that he under-estimated the flock-owners' income – particularly the income from meat sales.[2] According to my calculations, in order for an average shepherd to be enticed away from shepherding, he would need to see the chance of making at least 280 rupees a month; as well as to be compensated for the lack of milk and wool for his own use.

Shepherding is not easy. With today's problems added to the old, natural hazards, it is harder than ever before. Shepherds do not make a fortune. But in a part of the world where permanent employment is the privilege of a lucky few and a good cash crop is rare, it would be a brave shepherd who risked an alternative livelihood. It is true that many Kuluis have sold their flocks, but they are surrounded by examples of the possible cash return from investment in orchards. (And as Lyall pointed out many years ago, they never were as diligent or successful shepherds as the Gaddis.) Kulu is particularly well suited to fruit-growing. Perhaps fruit could grow well in Gadderan, too, but it would take some years to build a marketing infrastructure that could match those of Kulu, Kashmir and the area north of Simla. Kangra valley is too warm and wet for anything but lychees and mangoes, which would have to compete against the well-established, and earlier-fruiting, groves on the plains. As for angora-rabbit farming or bee-keeping ever being realistic alternatives to shepherding – let alone summer llama-grazing – the answer must be: never.

In Manali I met two brothers who reinforced my view that the Gaddis are likely to continue in their traditional calling. There is a Gaddi-owned grocery store in Manali, through which many Gaddis organize their rations. There I met Renu Ram, who invited me to visit him; he had two weeks' grazing in nearby Jugatsukh, rented from a Kului who had sold his flock. The large flock, of four hundred, were camped on a *tach* (pasture) just above the river, which was a lovely opaque green-blue in the autumn sunlight. Renu and his brother were both trimly barbered, well-built, middle-aged men, who exuded an air of being at ease with the world. I soon discovered why. Renu clicked his tongue with irritation when he found his watch was seven minutes late against mine. And it was easy to see he knew how to handle a pair of binoculars; though he was excited by the power of my pocket-sized ones. Both the brothers were used to keeping time and to modern pieces of personal equipment because, they explained, they had been military men. They were very well travelled; they had been stationed in Bihar, Calcutta and Assam. Renu had been in the army eighteen years and his brother fifteen. But they had retired to take over the flock when their father and uncle became too old for shepherding.

They had chosen to forgo the security of the relatively well paid military life to return and shepherd the family flock. Renu explained that there were four brothers in all, who had lived as a joint family. Now they had separated, but they still ran the flock jointly, all four taking a turn with it, and at the moment they had two nephews with them. Renu dexterously lit the cigarette which I had given him with a flint – a small piece of white quartz – and special dry, feathery grass from his brass *renuka* (tinder box). It was a very grand one with a delicately embossed pattern.

'Matches, for us they are no good. They get damp and the heads fly off and they are expensive. As long as you keep some of this grass dry somewhere these tinder boxes go on for ever. This one was my father's; he had it made for him at Tandi in Lahoul. Our young nephew bought a lighter in Manali bazaar the other day. It looked smart, it worked like magic for two days, he was very pleased. But then it was finished and so was his fifteen rupees.'

I tried to encourage him to talk about why he and his brother wanted to leave the army and come back to shepherding. Was it that they reckoned there was more money to be made from the flock than from continuing a military career?

I was not surprised at his evasive and dismissive reply.

'Oh no, no, we don't make much out of this life. But what could we do? Someone had to look after the flock when our father got too old. Our two younger brothers couldn't manage the fields at home and the flock as well. [It had not even been considered a possibility that the problem could be solved by the sale of the flock.] But it's a hard life; the young ones all want to go into service – the army, the government, and government offices. Look, all the way down through Kulu we'll be abused. There's nowhere but the river banks for the flocks, nowhere we can stay.'

'How about trucking the flock down?' I asked.

'It's very expensive. We did do it this spring when we had a lot of animals bad with sickness [foot and mouth disease] just from Patlikhul to Manali [20 km], to take them to the vet for injections. The truck cost us three hundred rupees, and the medicine didn't do any good. But, you understand, trucking wouldn't help; we would arrive at our winter place too early. The grazing there is little enough – if we reached there early it would be finished too soon.'

I was no more successful in encouraging him to expound on how the shepherds' problems could be solved or eased. Like most of those who feel victimized, he continued his complaints:

'Well, the forest people give us a lot of trouble. They close a jungle and we don't know it. Suddenly there is a fence around where we've always grazed. If we go in and the guard catches us he swears at us and gives us trouble until we buy him whisky and feed him with chickens. They are meant to tell us when they are going to close a jungle, and to give us somewhere else to go. In some places, where they've recently closed an area lying in the middle of our path, they say they have left a way through for us. That means they've closed it all except for a path so narrow you couldn't lead a dog through.

'We're told it's all for the good of the jungle, so there will be more timber. But the jungles have always been here and we've always been here. It's the Forest Department's own contractors who are cutting it all down and the guards give it cheap to villagers for bribes of whisky and money. But it is always we Gaddis who get the blame. Then they tell us we should give up goats and only keep sheep. What sort of sheep do they think can survive on the grazing we're left with?'

Renu does not consider his sheep and goats as the culprits responsible for a deteriorating environment. He smarts under what he considers unjust and endless harassment by the Forest Department. His indignation has some justification. I heard of a forest guard who himself drove a flock into an enclosed forest. Then he threatened to confiscate the trespassing flock and report the shepherds to the authorities unless they paid him two hundred rupees on the spot.

In Manali, to my surprise and delight, I found a letter from Sunni Devi. It was in Hindi, and did not say much; I wondered whom she had found to write it for her. She hoped the gods were blessing me and that I and my children were all right. Thanks to the *devi* they were all fine. They were about to leave Deori for the winter and she gave an address in Kangra. I was delighted. I had planned to move down towards the winter quarters with the shepherds but, having lost contact with Jagdish and Ram and Kapur Singh, I had been undecided where to head for. I would go and try to find Sunni Devi.

Karma and Tchering were loath to leave Manali: it was the marriage season and the big Dusshera fair was about to begin. We arranged that I would make my way on down the Kulu valley and we would meet some days later at Bajaura, then cross the Dulchi pass towards Kangra.

*

Kulu in October is extraordinarily pretty. As I wandered down the left bank of the Beas, I thought rice must be the most attractive of all cereals: the terraces were golden. Maize, already harvested, lay drying on the house roofs – a deeper orange.

Fresh snow made the skyline stand out against the azure blue sky. At midday, because of the hot sun, rivulets of snowmelt began to drain across the alps through the birch (some trees were bright yellow, others had already shed their leaves), and then further down the hill, growing into substantial streams, they dashed down rock faces – five hundred foot of white spray. They ran on, hidden by the dark forests of spruce and fir, into the magnificent deodar plantations. Towards the bottom of the steepest hillsides deodar still thin out naturally, and merge with the evergreen oaks on the scrubland. But much more often the dark deodars end in a trim horizontal band across the hill: they have been cut back by cultivators and orchard-owners extending their territory uphill.

The Beas has cut for itself a wide river bed. From high on the left bank I could not see the river, only a cleft in the valley floor. The apples had been harvested and their pale leaves added another yellow to the landscape. The villages are clustered on promontories, as though designed by a landscape architect. The houses are the finest in the west Himalayas. They are built of dry stone, dressed granite, bonded every four or five layers with horizontal lengths of deodar timber. Round this solid core is a veranda at an upper level, decorated with framed arches, fine trellis work and figurative carving.

But shepherds are not impressed by the colours and contours of the landscape. They are more concerned with dealing with harassment along the way – a skill which may have become as innate to them as a knowledge of the dangers of falling rocks and glaciers. Renu had told me how one of his goats had been chewing some succulent apple shoots over an orchard hedge. A muleteer who happened to be passing saw it and then saw the orchard owner kidnap the goat. If it had not been for the muleteer's information Renu would not have noticed that the goat was missing until he was well down the road, and would not have known where to begin looking. The orchard owner denied he had the goat. The muleteer kindly agreed to be a witness and to wait while Renu tried to fetch the police. Surprisingly they succeeded in bringing the police to the scene of altercation. The constable settled the case by insisting on the payment of some compensation for the orchard browsing, and on the return of the goat.

The difficulty of finding grazing and night halts along the way is not only due to 'reserved' forests and to Lahoulis, or Kuluis, enclosing land for orchards. Many of the shepherds' habitual camps used to be on government-owned 'waste' land. This is the land now often given as *nautor* – a gesture of land given to the landless by government policy. It also covers areas that have been given as camping grounds for Tibetan refugees, Nepali road labourers or the police and army. One of the shepherds' customary night halts has become a petrol station; another has been fenced off as a motel – land let to a big businessman for a small rent. And no provision has been made to find alternative night-halting places for the flocks.

Every autumn 140,000 migratory sheep and goats move down through Kulu. Some travel at night, to try to avoid the traffic. The oldest shepherd walks ahead; another, with the dogs, at the back, and the youngest acts as the runner here and there. No amount of horn-blowing by a vehicle trying to clear a path through the flock has any effect – not that this deters the driver from blasting his horn. I was in a bus caught behind a flock on a narrow stretch of road. The driver held his hand on the horn. Passengers made noises through their lips and whistled and banged the sides of the bus. The flock paid no need. Finally a passenger got out and walked straight up the bank calling in the shepherds' peculiar gutteral grunts: the flock followed him obediently.

Once I saw an over-impatient mini-van hit a sheep. I hardly saw what had happened before the old shepherd in the lead, without even glancing at the wounded sheep, stepped straight into the path of the accelerating van. It was forced to stop or run him over. And there he stood until his colleagues had assessed the damage to the sheep and he had successfully demanded compensation.

Not surprisingly, the shepherds are anxious to turn off the main Kulu valley as soon as possible – though where depends on their route to their winter grazing. The flocks' average daily stage is six to eight kilometres a day: through Kulu they may have had to do stages of double that distance to find somewhere to camp, let alone to graze. This takes its toll on the condition of the flock, and it is worse for those who travel up this way in the spring, when the animals are already weak.

Most now head up the side valleys to the right, crossing the most easterly, and lowest, spur of the Dhaula Dhar. Those whose winter pastures are near Sundernagar or Bilaspur must continue to follow the Beas. Unfortunate flocks, they have to brave the dusty rigours of the Larji-Mandi gorge road.

Karma and Tchering were waiting at Bajaura and we set off to the right, to cross the Dulchi pass towards Kangra valley and Palampur, to look for Sunni Devi.

1. Also to support this view, Bormann quoted Newall's claim that Gaddis were primarily agriculturalists and had only taken to shepherding when necessity demanded.
2. Bormann said that on an average ownership of 140 animals the income would be 5240 rupees per year; 1848 rupees of this was represented by

wool sales, leaving 3392 rupees from sales of meat. The latter figure
was based on an average of 200 rupees per animal. That is too low; even
in 1980 it was nearer 300, which would add another 1500 to the total.
If there were two men with the flock of 140 (though it is improbable
that two would be with the flock throughout the year), they would each
have an income of 3350, as well as milk from the goats and wool for
their family's use.

CHAPTER SEVEN

Opportunist Shepherds

Late autumn in Kangra

The little Dulchi pass (7500 feet) was a charming saddle through rhododendron and white-oak woods. The flock crossing ahead of us was held up as two nanny goats were giving birth. We camped just beyond the pass near some Gujars, and were treated to frothy buffalo milk and generous helpings of *ghi*.

The track ran almost parallel to the Larji-Mandi gorge road, but several thousand feet above, far from engine noise and dust. Far from the roaring river, too; the only sounds were ewes and nannies bleating for their young – the shepherds carried the newest born in the chest pouches of their *cholas*. I wandered along, revelling in the crisp, late-autumn air, feeling I had not a care in the world, and that, though the views among the big mountains are majestic and impressive, nothing could beat this. We made our way along the final ridge of the Dhaula Dhar and looked down across mile after mile and ridge after ridge, towards the head of Kangra valley and the jagged crests of the Sivalik hills.

The Dhaula Dhar range lies at a north-west to south-east angle. It divides the Upper Ravi valley and Gadderan, and then Barabangahal and the Kulu valley, from Kangra. Its most north-westerly extremity is just above Pathankot, where the Ravi river emerges from the hills of Chamba and flows into the plains of the Punjab. Here we were at its most south-easterly spur, where it is narrowest and lowest – cut through by the Larji-Mandi gorge.

Shepherds' migrational routes are dictated by the location of their summer and winter pastures. Those who spend the winter at the western end of the winter grazing grounds took high, westerly passes from Lahoul across the main Himalayas, and by now must have been moving towards Pathankot and Nurpur. Those who headed east from Kulu, towards Bilaspur and Kalka, were the ones who had to brave the horrors of the gorge road. It was to avoid the higher passes across the Dhaula Dhar, and the danger of autumn snow, that hundreds of flocks came down through Kulu; and, like us, many were crossing the narrowest spur by the low routes above Mandi, and then turning west to Kangra. Fortunate shepherds who own land in Kangra may spend several weeks on the southern slopes of the range, above the villages, in the forests and glades near Jogindernagar, Baijnath and Palampur.

'I have heard old shepherds say that down to British rule it was like running the gauntlet to convey a flock across the low country to its *ban* [winter grazing]. Every petty official or influential landowner tried to extort something as the flock passed him. A mild man was easily daunted and had no chance so the Gaddis picked out their ugliest customers for the work,' wrote J. B. Lyall in the late 1860s.[1] Perhaps the old shepherd I had seen stepping out into the path of the accelerating van was a descendant of one of those 'ugly customers'. A hundred years ago, as now, to be a successful shepherd it was not enough to have an eye for sheep and good grazing: you had to be tough. It may be that Gaddis have survived, while so many other transhumant people have been forced to abandon their traditional livelihood, just because they do have that toughness and an astute opportunism.

The Beas river has to take a loop to skirt the Dhaula Dhar, then, after the little market town of Mandi, it turns again to its natural westerly direction towards the Indus. Its valley is known as Kangra (though, because the geological formation of the Sivaliks is so complicated, it is hardly recognizable as a valley), until it leaves Himachal and enters the Punjab.

We came down off the ridge at Jathingri on our way to Baijnath. Kangra, at an average height of two to three thousand feet, is very different from the valleys of the higher hills. In the valleys further into the mountains, nature's ferocity only just tolerates man's intrusion. There the villages, terraces and paths are precarious: at any moment intolerance may burst forth – as an avalanche, a landslide or a river which devastatingly changes its course. But here men and nature live together harmoniously. The terraced fields of the valley floor are broad and well watered, by the high rainfall and by the snow-melt cascading down from the Dhaula Dhar: they regularly bear two crops a year.

The landscape is delightful. It has an un-Indian, almost European proportion, something of a Constable painting, which is soothing to the senses. Houses are not clustered together as in the high hills, but placed here and there among the fields, shaded by large trees and stands of bamboo. A large joint family has a considerable dwelling built round three sides of a courtyard, and separate buildings, in the same style, for the cattle. They are built of stone below and brick above, mud-plastered and sometimes washed with a pink ochre. The roofing slates are black and very tidy. From the front the buildings have the look of a child's drawing, neat and well proportioned; shallow-ridged roofs and small square windows, which are dark, as there is no glass to reflect the light. And the back-cloth to the scene is the White Range – the Dhaula Dhar.

'In other parts of the Himalayas the effect of the snowy mountains is softened, if not injured, by the intermediate ranges; and the mind is gradually prepared by a rising succession of hills for the stupendous heights which terminate the scene. But in Kangra there is nothing to intercept the view. The lower hills appear by comparison like ripples on the surface of the sea, and the eye rests uninterrupted on a chain of mountains which attain an absolute elevation of 13,000 feet above the valleys spread out at their base. Few spots in the Himalayas for beauty and grandeur can compete with the Kangra Valley and these over-shadowing hills.'[2]

Our arrival at Baijnath meant that our journey had completed a full circle. It was from here on that May morning that we had caught the bus to Binwa and the squalor of the hydel project, before starting on our first day's walk. The address Sunni Devi had written said 'Palampur *tehsil* [district]', which was a little further to the east. First I wanted to call at Kapur Singh's home; he had told me his parents' address during a card-playing afternoon in Miyar *nala*.

There are Gaddi families scattered in villages throughout Kangra, but the greatest concentration of them live at the foot of the mountains along the rim of the valley from Joginder-nagar to below Dharamsala. These villages are not exclusively Gaddi – Kangris live there, too. In spite of the sense of well-being that Kangra emanates, it is in fact seriously over-populated. The density of population was already a cause of anxiety to administrators in the mid-nineteenth century and is now well above the level considered possible for the support of that population.[3] Despite the fertile soil and the kind climate, holdings are too small to grow enough for the family. Most households survive only because some men go away – to the army, to become servants, mechanics or joiners – and send cash back home. If Kangra is over-populated, and already was in the mid-nineteenth century, how was it that Gaddis were able to come in and establish themselves here and are continuing to do so today?

It was partly owing to Lyall's role as settlement officer in Kangra in the 1860s and his particular enthusiasm for the Gaddis that they had the chance to establish themselves here and acquire grazing rights on the southern slopes of the Dhaula Dhar. Shepherds who have those rights are at an advantage. They can break the journey from the summer to the winter pastures with an autumn sojourn, and do so again in the spring. It gives the flocks and the shepherds a badly needed rest from the rigours of being on the move, and means less time has to be spent at the overcrowded and scanty winter pastures.

A man ploughing a wide terrace directed me to Kapur Singh's home. I walked on through the terraces towards the village five hundred feet above Baijnath. Flocks were enjoying a feed on the maize stubble, and manuring the ground before the winter ploughing. The village houses here on the rim of the valley were more compactly grouped than those below; probably to conserve all available land for cultivation, rather than in a conscious effort to re-create replicas of the villages in Gadderan. The earliest Gaddis to settle here built their own houses; the older ones have noticeably more timber, and verandas on the upper floor. Today's are built by Kangra carpenters in conventional Kangra style, with balconies as extensions of windows rather than running the full length of the house. Village taps spouted pipe water and every house had an electricity wire trailing from it. In the courtyards the house-shrines and *tulsi* (basil) plants were well tended – signs of traditional Hindu households.

I found the house and the old couple. They had not had word from Kapur. They were pleased to have news and relieved that when I had last seen him, all was well with him and the flock. The old man, Kapur's father and Jagdish's elder brother, had eyes that never rested on anything in the foreground, as though their focus was permanently set at the distance of a far hillside. He was probably not more than fifty-five but had an air of venerable age, reinforced by his lack of interest in his appearance; his *chola* was tattered to rags. We sat beside the loom in their 'public' room, downstairs. It was hung about with wool, spun balls of it, grey and white, and basketfuls yet to be carded. A four-year-old granddaughter played with a clay doll in the corner and a toddler was proudly displayed as the first son of the next generation.

The family still felt an association with their original home at Nayagraon in the Upper Ravi. A third brother – or perhaps he was a cousin – lived there still, and Kapur's father crossed the Jalsu pass to spend the summers there. I asked when they had first acquired property in Kangra. 'They say it was my grandfather's grandfather who bought land here. In those days they had big flocks, maybe twenty *tols* [a *tol* is forty in local usage]. So he had plenty of gold; he bought the land.'

No casual enquirer would have imagined that this old man's great-great-grandfather could have been an opportunist land-grabber. But by now I had become aware that the Gaddis' 'rustic', tribal appearance belied their character. It was not until after this journey, when I re-read the old *Gazetteers* and *Settlement Reports*, that the story jumped out at me from the brittle, yellow and often silverfish-eaten pages.

Even four or five generations ago the Gaddis had been oppor-
tunists: they had had the nous to buy land at a period of social
and administrative change. Also I realized that the story of
how it became possible for them to acquire land here in
Kangra was an intriguing illustration of the energy and
meticulousness of some of the early British administrators;
sometimes their work did alter the status quo, with a lasting
effect. In this case the result was to be a continuing benefit to
the Gaddi shepherds. I found it an interesting story, and to
appreciate the Gaddis' position today, both geographically
and economically, it needs to be understood. Their difficulties,
their aims and their character become clearer if they are seen
in the context of what happened a hundred years ago.

Until the middle of the nineteenth century the Raja of
Kangra (as in the other hill states) had been the sole owner of
all land. The cultivator could only be a tenant: his right was
only to use the land, though the tenancy might have been
inherited for many generations. The same system applied to
grazing rights; pastures were leased from the Raja and, as
with cultivated land, the grazing tenancy could be inherited
and also sub-let. In 1846 the British defeated the Sikh empire
and annexed its territory, which included Kangra, Kulu and
Lahoul. The British brought in their experienced land settlement officers. It was their duty to discover who were the
'rightful tenants' to every plot. For the first essential was to
establish who were the ones who would have to pay revenue;
the next to compile reliable records, essential for the settlement of land – or revenue – disputes. So every patch of cultivatable land had to be delineated and its cultivator identified.
It was no easy task.

The first settlement officer in Kangra was a Mr C. G. Barnes.
He became so well liked by the people of his district that there
were murmurs within the administration (later proved un-
founded) that his popularity must be due to an over-lenient

assessment of the revenue taxes. He wrote a vivid account of the days and weeks he spent with the villagers out among the terraces. When everyone had gathered round, to voice their claims and to witness the demonstration of British efficiency, his assistant, the *kanbah* (so called because he wielded a bamboo *kan* – pole), would measure out the land.

'The *kanbah* when employed in measurement stands upon the edge of the field and grasping the bamboo in both hands, swings it forward like an angler does a rod, bringing the top to descend upon the ground, where it leaves a slight mark. The measurer then walks rapidly up to this spot, and repeats the process until the entire length of the field is measured out. There is no halting or delay. The measurer walks at a steady and uninterrupted pace, and the bamboo is seen to descend regularly before him making out the path that he is to follow.'[4]

The next settlement officer was Lyall. He made the picturesque *kanbah* redundant and instead taught his assistants the use of the chain and plane table. (Even today all land transactions are settled by the *patwari* out in the field measuring it with a chain, length by length, and references to the old settlement records are often necessary.)

It was a hard task to establish who was the 'rightful tenant' in each case. Often it was not the present cultivator, since so much of the land was subdivided and sublet. Many of the arguments were over who held the hereditary right to the tenancy. But when the 'rightful tenants' were identified, the British Raj decided they were to become absolute owners. This was the important innovation: as owners rather than tenants, they could now, if they wanted, sell the land. The British created a potential land market here where it had never existed before.

Because Gaddi shepherds and their flocks had always passed through Kangra on their way to and from their winter pastures, it is likely that there were some with a toe-hold here before the 1860s and 1870s. Now, using cash accumulated from their flocks, many, like Kapur Singh's great-great-great-grandfather, were able to to take advantage of the new land market. Few others besides Gaddis possessed the necessary cash. Traditionally, village cultivators in these hills have subsisted off their land. Sometimes they have been able to buy additional food and necessities with small sums earned from labouring, but even an army wage did not (and does not) provide enough surplus cash to buy land. In the rural districts the only people with cash have been traders, money-lenders and the shepherds.

For the shepherds, whose homes and fields were in Gadderan, on the other side of the Dhaula Dhar, the attraction of buying land here was more than just the acquisition of a plot to build on or to cultivate. The real advantage was that with the ownership of cultivated land went grazing rights on the village 'waste land' – extensive areas of hillside. So sought after were these grazing rights that early this century the incoming shepherds were buying patches of land at such inflated prices that it caused local resentment. The British administrators, who had been responsible for creating the situation, took the line that it was no good the villagers raising a hue and cry about the incoming Gaddis. It was the proprietors' own fault, who greedy for high prices had sold to outsiders.

Arguments about grazing rights, and rightful inheritors, were as complex and contentious as those about the rights to cultivated land. So much so that, had Lyall not had such an interest in the Gaddis and not been so energetic on their behalf, it is improbable that the grazing issues would have been settled as well as they were. He took considerable trouble to master all the customs and the complexities involved, because he believed British fair play demanded it.[5] As I read I began to realize that he was not just the first; he was the *only* person who acquired a detailed knowledge about the migratory shepherds. All the information in later *Gazetteers*, and even the material in more recent works, consists really of Lyall's observations, abridged and often unacknowledged.

Lyall's enthusiasm led him to make the arduous two-week journey over to Lahoul, which involved struggling over two 13,000-foot passes. And his interest engendered a protective and paternal attitude. His predecessor, Barnes, had decreed that both the Gujar buffalo herdsmen and the shepherds should pay their grazing rights to the local villagers. Lyall decided that the Gaddis should pay them to the state. In so doing he ensured that they became direct tenants of the British Raj. In other words he established them in a position that demanded a degree of paternal protection.[7] It might well have been construed as favouritism. Every now and then the level-headed British administrators were accused of favouring a particular caste, tribe or religion. I find Lyall's role very sympathetic. In his position I would probably have acted as he did; my interest in the Gaddis has grown into a strong affection.

Before we moved on to Palampur, I visited a Gaddi ex-Member of Himachal's Parliament, the State Legislative Assembly, which meets in Simla. He had been the member for Bramour's reserved constituency. I walked up from Palampur towards Bandla village. Shri Ram Chand's house was just below the village. It was a well-appointed bungalow – glass windows, a semi-enclosed courtyard at the back, and at the front a concrete platform shaded by trees. We sat on the platform drinking instant coffee (more fashionable than tea). As well as the establishment here, he retained another on the far side of the Dhaula Dhar. And, like Kapur Singh's family, he referred to his connection with his original village. Kangra-based Gaddis consider Gadderan their cultural home. They regard it rather in the same way as third-generation Glasgow-born Highlanders feel about their original home in the Highlands or Islands of Scotland: it is where the soul belongs.

The ex-MLA said that, though some families had been settled here for four or five generations, Kangra Gaddis remained a separate community from their Kangra neighbours. He claimed, though I knew it was not strictly true, that Gaddi Brahmins married only among themselves, whether from this or the far side of the Dhaula Dhar, but not among Kangra Brahmins.

'But, yes, we have picked up fashions from here. A desire for radios and watches and tin trunks and showy marriages – there must be fancy food, something sweet, something sour, and it is important who sits where. In Gadderan we were a simple lot: it didn't matter who was who, or what you ate, as long as there was something to drink to help the singing and the dancing. But here everyone asks your caste and so we've grown more conscious of it; it's a fashion.

'And then there is the dowry business. We Gaddis didn't know about it. We used to give money sometimes in order to get a good hard-working girl for our sons. But now amongst us in Kangra that is changing: people are beginning to give money with their daughters like the Punjabi people. That is not good; it is like selling your daughter.'

From what I had gathered in Gadderan, Kangra associations were important when arranging marriages. Girls preferred not to be married into a family who did not have a home, or at least relatives to winter with, in Kangra. And a Kangra-based girl would be unlikely to agree to marry into a family from the remote Budil valley with no Kangra connection. Dowry consciousness and the social attitudes associated with it have moved fast. Many hill communities, which in the past have thought in terms of the importance of finding a good hard-working girl for their sons, now think in terms of getting a good match for their daughters; whether or not they actually pay a dowry price. (Later I was to have the feeling that one of Sunni Devi's most urgent reasons for wanting to buy a patch of land in Kangra was to improve the marriage prospects for her two daughters.)

Shri Ram Chand's daughter was about to be married. In spite of his claimed disapproval of dowries, I was sure he was paying one, but thought it would be tactless to ask. I admired the bride's trousseau and the beautifully made *luancharis*. In the courtyard at the back of the house the women were weaving rush mats, and blankets were soaking in troughs and pails with 'soap' from the soap-nut tree. Both the matting and the blankets would be laid out in lines for the wedding guests to sit on. *Luancharis* were being 'pressed' – they were hanging from trees, a cord binding the waist and hem of each one to press the pleats. And the palanquin was being repaired. The bride would be carried in it, sobbing, from her paternal home:

> O Mother Dhaulidhar
> Bend a little,
> Oh bend a little.
> On this side lies my mother-in-law's home,
> On the other side lies my father's home,
> Bend yourself a little,
> Bend a little.
> On the marriage day in a palanquin
> My brother gave me a farewell –
> 'Bathe in milk, blossom in sons!'
> My brother's wife blessed me,
> My mother gave me tears.
> Bend yourself a little,
> Bend a little,
> Oh bend a little.[8]

*

On my way back down from his house I passed fields where Nepali labourers were preparing the ground for winter wheat. I asked whose fields they were. 'A Gaddi Brahmin's,' was the answer. 'Who else but Gaddis can afford to hire labourers to till all the land they've bought?' The old resentment against the in-comers still continues; though generally Gaddis are regarded as good neighbours, they cause some jealousy among their neighbours. Sheep and goats continue to provide the cash for land purchases. During the last twenty-five years, flock-owning Gaddis have been able to buy much more land than those who have no flocks. They have been able to increase the area of cultivated land which they inherited by more than twenty-five per cent.[9]

Tchering and I had dinner in Palampur's only glass-fronted restaurant. Karma had left us and gone to visit some relations. It was an excuse, I knew. He was uncomfortable trailing Gaddis in the bazaars and villages of Kangra. It was all right in the hills, where it was more in keeping with his usual trekking-guide role, but he felt ill at ease wandering about here. A group of the customers wanted to know why I had been in the villages up in the hills, so far from the main road. I tried to explain my interest. I gathered from their reaction that they regarded Gaddis, with slight condescension, as country bumpkins. But when, during the course of our conversation, I asked them about local land prices, they sighed. 'Oh, no one can buy rice or maize land round here. Only Khampa traders and the Gaddi shepherds can afford it and it's they who have pushed up the prices.'

1. J. B. Lyall, *Settlement Report*.
2. J. B. Lyall, *Punjab District Gazetteer 1906*.
3. 1900 people to the square mile. Jonathan Parry, *Caste and Kinship in Kangra*.

4. G. C. Barnes, *Settlement Report.*

5. '. . . previous ignorance has caused wrong decisions and bad feeling, bad administration and bad law enforcements.'

6. He was impressed by the shepherding skills of the Gaddis: 'I have often admired the Gaddi shepherd; he knows every sheep or goat out of a flock of many hundred by sight and has a name for him founded on some peculiarity indistinguishable by other eyes but his own. He soon misses one which has strayed just as a captain might miss a soldier of his company. . . . The Gaddi shepherds are much more careful and energetic shepherds than the Kolis [largely Kuluis]; they may be seen herding their goats in the face of tremendous precipices. . . . Their sheep are reputed strong and hardy above those of any other shepherds.' J. B. Lyall, *Settlement Report.*

7. 'The Deputy Commissioner in his executive capacity should, in my opinion, look after the interests of these shepherds in case of quarrels with the village communities, for in respect of grazing rights they are tenants of the state. . . .' J. B. Lyall, *Settlement Report.*

8. Quoted by M. S. Randhawa in *Travels in the Western Himalayas.*

9. R. P. Phillimore, 'Marriage and Social Organisation among Pastoralists of the Dhaula Dhar'.

CHAPTER EIGHT

A Visit to Sunni Devi's Family

Winter

The address Sunni Devi had sent said care of the *sarpanch* (head of the village council) of Parar village but, according to my map, the name referred to an area, or a collection of villages rather than a particular one. Surprisingly, amongst the disorganized squalor of Palampur's bus station, it took a mere ten minutes to establish the bus route. The last part of the instructions the booking clerk gave us were vague and included a walk of an hour or more. Once out of the bus, we were faced with a choice of a path to the right or one to the left, and I suddenly felt it was improbable that I would find her.

It was a beautiful morning. New snow on the Dhaula Dhar gave the mountains the veneer of having been created the night before. Where the cliffs and ridges were too sheer for snow to lie the granite itself broke through. And a fresh dusting of snow covered the dark forested skirts of the mountains. The air was soft. To the south there was a large expanse of deep blue sky, giving the sense of space you never feel when right up in the hills. Here the terraces were wide and gently graded; pale green with winter wheat, darker under the shade of trees, which had been planted like a park. There were bauhinias, flame of the forest and sixty-foot stands of bamboo (five different types grow in Kangra). In the neat gardens, round the neat mud-plastered houses, there were nasturtiums and geraniums in pots, and roses grew beside the railway crossing.

We had walked, slowly enjoying the morning, for four or five kilometres when we interrupted a woman who was patterning the walls of her house with dung cakes (to dry for fuel). Yes, the *sarpanch's* house was on down the path and off to the left. It was a substantial establishment built round three sides of a courtyard. A line of cattle – cows and buffaloes and their calves – and three spotted goats munched leafy branches from a trough. The courtyard was decorated with designs in white chalk, and on the steps there were rosettes made out of *tulsi* plant leaves. A woman, and many children, emerged from a door to the right. We explained we were looking for Sunni Devi, a Gaddini: no reaction. From a door further to the right (I had assumed it was a byre or a goat shed), there appeared a scruffy old Gaddini. I asked, enthusiastically, 'Sunni Devi, from Deori village? Does she live here? She is a Gaddini from Deori near Holi.'

It seemed that my earlier forebodings about the chances of finding her were coming true. The expression on the women's faces or, rather, the lack of expression made it clear that not a word I said meant anything to them. She was away? Or, worse, it was the wrong village? Or Sunni Devi had moved her winter lodgings? There could be so many reasons for not finding her here. I had not thought about what I would do if she was not living here, and I sat in the sun to absorb the disappointment.

One of the expressionless women had gone into the building on the other side of the courtyard, as though to call for help. An imposing, elderly man wearing a Lahouli hat summoned me over. 'Sunni Devi? Yes, yes, she'll be back in the evening.

173

Come along in.' We were led into a sparkling white-washed room with glazed windows, surely not Sunni Devi's. The titles of the books on the shelves and open on the table suggested that it belonged to a student of chemistry. A youth in white *kurta* and pyjama brought in the tea: it was his room. The *sarpanch*, his father, explained that he knew all about me.

'You're the one who goes away over the mountains to Deori. You gave Sunni Devi a watch. It's stopped going now. No one can make it work. Yes, she lives here, she's been coming here for the winter for years. She does spinning and weaving. She's gone to relations to help at a delivery; she should be back before dark. You just wait here with us.'

I saw the girls – Munni and her sister, whom I had last seen at Deori – giggling at the window, but when I reached the door they had fled. I couldn't wait, but I left a sticky brown paper bag of *jelebis* for them and promised to come back the next day.

Next morning we took a short cut through the *chil* pine forest. Sunni Devi was there: she was brought into the student's room. We embraced and she settled herself on the floor beside the plastic-covered sofa where I had been told to sit. But we did not stay there long. She signalled she wanted me to leave and led me round the back of the *sarpanch*'s bungalow and into her windowless five-feet-by-six-feet room. Most of it was taken up by wool: balls of spun wool hung from the ceiling, there were baskets of recently carded wool on the floor, raw wool in goatskin bags, newly woven blankets hanging from ropes and a *chakra* spinning wheel behind the door. In the little space that remained she lived with her two daughters and little Soban. It was immaculate. The floor was a dark khaki green from the cow-dung wash. And now, before lighting the fire with the thinnest of twigs ('It's so difficult here, there's no wood, it's not like at home'), she gave the *chulha* a wipe over with cow dung and water.

We were lucky to find her because she had been with her husband and brothers and their flocks at their winter grazing down at Dehri on the Beas, but had just come back as she had not been well – she was suffering from boils and a fever. The room, even the doorway, was soon jammed with people. Steel *thalis* piled with rice, vegetables and dal were brought for us by one of the many women. I hardly had the space to place the *thali* on the floor in front of me and to cross my legs to eat. The *sarpanch's* establishment obviously incorporated several households; they were all Kangra women – no sign of the bedraggled Gaddini from the day before. The chemistry student sat beside me and some space was made for his mother and sister. Though they were a Brahmin family, and well to do, they treated Sunni and her children with an unusual lack of contempt, looked her in the eye and joked with her. And they also joined in the lengthy discussion about what to do with the watch that would not go. At the moment it was with her nephew, a student at college in Hamirpur (in Kangra) because he had suggested he could take it to Goa to be mended when he went on a college trip next year. I suppose it was thought that Goa was so far away that Goanese watch-makers were bound to be able to mend it.

Sunni Devi had been making *halwa* and Munni had been sent to milk the goat for some tea. We and the chemistry student and his mother and sister were served with biscuits, multi-coloured meringues of puffed-up rice – pink, yellow and white, and the *halwa*, which is a rich and expensive dish of semolina fried in *ghi* with nuts and raisins. I had had a substantial breakfast in Palampur bazaar, had done justice to the *thali*-ful of rice and was embarrassed by this expenditure on my account, because I knew that what I left on my plate would not be given to those who had not had any, not even to the children: it would be *jutha*, made unclean by another's touch.

175

The room had become warm. In the *sarpanch*'s tidy garden the sun glowed on the nasturtiums.

I wanted to photograph Sunni Devi at her loom, in the shed behind the line of buffaloes and goats. It was not the conventional pit loom, but a frame loom with the advantage of a flying shuttle. But weaving is still time-consuming: the loom is only wide enough for half the warp to be set on it; later, the two halves are sewn together. The result is an attractive blanket, with the large black, or brown, and white squares set off by a red seam down the middle. It takes two kilos, or three if it is a large one, of spun wool to weave a blanket. The final product is sold for three or four hundred rupees. Sunni Devi does some weaving for villagers who bring in their wool. More often she sells the blankets she weaves with her own wool. The work provides her with cash to help with the daily expenses of rent, food and clothes. And I had the feeling it also allows her a degree of financial independence. Her husband must know how many fleeces she retains after the autumn and winter shearing, but cannot estimate accurately how much she can prepare and weave, nor find out the exact sale price.

The economics of such a home industry are not easy to establish. Not only because someone like Sunni Devi is loath to give specific answers, but also because she does not calculate time spent at this work in terms of earning money. During the winter she, and many other Gaddini, may occasionally spend more or less a whole day spinning and weaving. Much more often the laborious cleaning, carding and spinning, more time-consuming than the weaving, is done intermittently between other household chores. So an average day's production depends on whether she has to go for firewood, or take grain to the mill; and, conversely, on how many visitors call, who, while they gossip, help with the cleaning, carding and spinning.

Carding in particular hinders fast progress; and how well wool is carded has an important effect on the quality of the spun wool. There is a carding machine in Palampur but – and I have heard the same view in other places in the hills – Sunni Devi says: 'It's not worth the trouble of going there. You have to carry all your wool there, and when you get there often it's not working and if it is you still have to waste time waiting your turn. And the machines don't do the carding work properly.' When Sunni Devi sells a blanket at her top price of 400 rupees, she earns herself, at a very rough estimate, 9 rupees for an eight-hour day's work: if she sells it for 300, she earns nearer 5 rupees. [1]

The economics of domestic wool manufacture was not a subject I could discuss with Sunni Devi as we walked up the road; it was too much for our halting Hindi, and Tchering had gone to the temple with the chemistry student. Even later, when he was around to interpret, the concept was too theoretical for her to absorb, or even to interest her. But as she described her difficulties in making ends meet, it seemed to me very relevant.

'You see, I have to pay a lot of rent to the *sarpanch*, and the children must have clothes. If only I could buy land here; crops never grow well at Deori, there's not enough water. If I could get four or five *karnals* here, we could have a house and grow vegetables. But with a flock of only a *tol*, we'll never get the money. My brother bought land, eleven *karnals*, here last year but he has three or four *tols*.'

It was then that she mentioned how, if they had land, it would also help when the time came to arrange marriages for her two daughters.

Sunni Devi had agreed that the next day she would take us down to Dehri to meet her husband and brothers and their flocks. There had been a lengthy discussion on how to get there. She felt sick in the bus. 'How did you come back from there the other day?' I asked. 'On the bus; I was sick all the way.' It seemed the bus was the quickest way to cover the fifty miles or so – there was a direct one from Palampur that stopped at her road end. And I could buy travel sickness medicine. She was not enthusiastic: 'The train is better.' But it was too far for her to walk to Palampur station, and there was no bus to Palampur so early in the morning. Then there was another problem: if we were to stay with the flock for some days, she could not leave little Soban behind. If she brought him, he was no good at walking and would be too heavy to carry. Soban made it clear he had no intention of being left behind.

Perhaps Sunni Devi had thought better of the expedition and hoped, by posing problems, to dissuade me from the idea. For much time and discussion had passed before she expressed what apparently was to her the major stumbling block to the whole expedition: 'If you stay there how will you sleep? There aren't any *charpois*; we sleep on the ground. And what will you eat? There'll just be *makki ki roti* [maize chapattis] and milk of course.'

I tried to reassure her: I was used to the ground, I had a sleeping bag, I liked *makki ki roti* and even sometimes ate them at home in preference to ordinary chapattis. I do not think she was convinced, but ultimately it was agreed that she would walk across the fields to her local station and we would come by bus from Palampur to the nearest roadhead, walk on down and meet her at the station at 7.30 a.m.

At six o'clock the very battered bus lurched down through Palampur bazaar. The tattered brocade curtains flapped out of the windows, taped movie music screeched and the images of Shivji and Ganesh, suspended above the windscreen, danced in front of the driver – I hoped they augured well for our expedition.

It was cold so early in the morning. We found Sunni Devi and little Soban and a plump niece huddled under black-and-white check blankets on a railway bench. They had been waiting for more than an hour, having left home at dawn. I was eagerly looking forward to the journey, but they did not seem to be. I began to feel guilty: maybe I had imposed the expedition on them. Now Soban had a fever, as well as Sunni Devi – I had brought penicillin for her boils and had some Dispirin with me. We went to the railway tea stall, for water to wash down the Dispirin and in the hope of engendering some cheer with hot tea and biscuits. Inside there was a Gaddi couple. They must have been on their way to attend a marriage, for the woman was hardly visible under a wealth of ornaments – an elaborately decorated headcloth, hair jewellery and chains, nose- and ear-rings, necklaces, both gold and silver, and a pendant depicting Shiva and Parvati in crude blue enamelling. She was also wearing an immaculately pleated new *luanchari*.

It seemed that the train was the Gaddis' preferred means of transport, for we were to see many others during the morning's journey. It may be that, like Sunni Devi, Gaddis chose the *rel gari* (train) rather than the 'motor', as they call the bus, out of fear of motor sickness. Whatever the reason, their choice is the right one. Buses career along between roadsides made sordid with mechanics' workshops and second-hand tyre shops, and stop, at the driver's pleasure, at squalid bus stands. Our train, on the other hand, meandered through terraced fields and *chil* pine woods, through cuttings and over viaducts and stopped just long enough to buy a bowl (made from leaves) full of spicy *pakora* at the trim, unhurried stations.

I was ecstatic with pleasure: it was one of those rare moments when you feel yourself to be an integral part of a harmonious universe; apprehensions, anxieties and the grinding of ill-tuned gears have no meaning; fleetingly you cannot envisage anything ever going wrong. Even Tchering, who had barely disguised his envy of Karma's escape, enjoyed the experience. Sunni Devi and Soban had both cheered up – perhaps the Dispirin had worked – and the plump niece had relaxed into the pleasure of travel. She and Soban were guzzling bananas and oranges. There was room in the wooden-benched carriage to move from one side to the other (both had windows) and you could also stand at the open door.

On our right, up above, the magnificent Dhaula Dhar shone white. At one moment our carriage would be darkened by a *chil* pine forest right up to the windows; at the next, as we came out into the open, we were dazzled by sunlight. Fields were pale green with wheat; violent yellow with mustard; rich brown where potatoes were newly planted. There were oleanders, flame of the forest, bombax trees, acacias and sumachs. Looking out from a train (especially from this one where the windows were small and framed; not like the plate-glass expanses in an inter-city express) is like watching a slide show. You cannot see ahead so you are constantly surprised by visual contrasts – the vast panoramas and then the close-ups, the light and then the shade. And when I leaned out of the doorway (we did not travel at speed), I could see the tail of the train, curling this way and that behind us. There must have been a marriage party aboard, for it was flamboyantly decorated with bougainvillaeas and roses – scarlet, pink and orange.

Suddenly Kangra fort towered above us. Its extensive though ruined battlements were hardly distinguishable from its natural fortifications – the massive bulk of sedimentary rock on which it stands. No wonder that for many centuries it was so strategically important. It was sacked by Mahmud of Ghazna in 1009 (its fall and the subsequent persecutions making this one of the eras when the Gaddis fled north into the hills of Bramour), then rose to importance and power again under the Moghuls; but its heyday was during the reign of Sansar Chand, the greatest of the rajas of Kangra, in the late eighteenth century. The fort is made yet more impressive by its position above the gorge of the Ban Ganga river. Great buttresses of conglomerate rock rose up out of the river bed.

The geology of the Himalayas is testing even for the professionals. A casual student cannot hope to master the results of 'subductions of oceanic lithospheres', but the Sivalik range in Kangra (much of it confusingly called Kangra valley) is so arresting that it is impossible to pass through without comment. The Indian plate, which detached itself from Gondwana and some fifty million years ago thrust itself under Tibet, creating the Himalayas, has continued to penetrate into Asia at a rate of 5 centimetres a year. So the Himalayas are still growing. As they do so the crust of the Indian plate gets sliced off, leaving newly emerged rock on the southern side. The Sivaliks, named after Lord Shiva, are the result of a comparatively new boundary fault, caused by the weight of the Himalayas on the strong plate of North India. As the Himalayas have continued to slide over India they have folded and faulted the sedimentary rocks at their foot. The youngest of the sedimentary rocks are the conglomerates brought down by eroding glaciers and rivers. 'The Sivalik sediments are ploughed into folds and thrust on top of one another and are over-thrust by the older rocks of the Lesser Himalaya.'[2] No wonder the Kangra landscape is so confusing.

I was still dwelling on the complexity of the area's geology when we drew up at a station and Sunni Devi hurled her blanket bundles through the window on to the platform. From here we were to catch a bus to the pilgrimage town of Jawalaji (famous for its temple, which has an everlasting flame) and there change buses.

*

181

I imagine the shepherds have always felt ill at ease during the winter; but over the past decades their situation has become worse. Set against their winter terrain they appear uncomfortable and incongruous. As our bus trundled down the dusty track from Jawalaji, I saw a shepherd striding along across the short midday shadows under an avenue of mango trees. The temperature must have been in the nineties, but he was in full dress – a tweed *chola*, kilted with a heavy *dora* – his hill stick was in his hand and he was followed by a panting dog. He looked as out of place as would a Highlander in a kilt and plaid in a leafy Surrey lane in July.

One o'clock found our little group of travellers sheltering from the midday heat under the trailing roots of a banyan tree, on the banks of the Beas. Here the river languorously makes it way across wide gravel banks; very different from the confined and turbulent torrent of the upper Kulu valley. A little way downstream we could see some sheep and goats but Sunni Devi said they were local. Her flocks were the other side of the river. Our buoyant mood of the train journey had gone: it was Dispirin time again for both Sunni Devi and Soban.

She said that beyond the roadhead, here at the river, we would have to walk. The prospect had not worried me. I had imagined it might be a couple of miles to the shepherds' camp.

We dragged ourselves out into the sunlight and crossed the river on a bridge of country boats tethered together side by side (a signboard gave the toll charges, which included a price for a tiger in a cage and a body on a bier). Having staggered up the steep path on the far side, we rested again in the shade: now it became clear that it was not a simple question of a two-mile walk to the camp. No one knew where it was. The niece asked a Gaddi who was leading or, rather, pushing a couple of goat kids down the hill if he had seen Munshi Ram and his flock. From his answering expression it was clear he had no idea. An elderly woman walking home alone from a bazaar claimed she had a vague idea of the direction and we walked on together. But as time passed I began to wonder whether she had not made her claim because she saw an opportunity for company on her long walk home.

We walked for four hours, along tracks through prickly scrub jungle, across dusty pastures or patches that had been intended to be wheat fields – it was hard to tell. From above or from the roadside you might assume this was waste land; territory which would be described as 'marginal', being neither agricultural nor forest. It is on land like this that the flocks must spend at least four months – from the end of November to the end of March – maybe longer. And it is the poor quality and quantity of grazing here that has always limited both the numbers of flocks and their size.

Lyall noticed that the winter pastures were already under pressure in the 1850s and 1860s. He said the *bans* had little grass, and what there was was dry and coarse; most of the grazing consisted of the thorny shrub *Carissa diffusa* and the rank plant *Justicia adhatoda*. Here goats suffer less than sheep; the latter do not enjoy a diet of prickly shrubs, they lose wool on the thorny bushes, and in the heat they huddle together and are reluctant to graze properly.[3]

Today the shepherds' situation is worse than it was a hundred years ago, partly because shepherds who succeeded in establishing their right to a run at the end of the last century have since bred a dozen grandchildren. Some or all of these may be flock-owners and assume that they have inherited a right to a grazing. Another cause of hard feeling is that when flock-owners pay the annual tax to the Forest Department they assume that it automatically entitles them to grazing, while the Forest Department takes the view that it is only a tax, not a licence to graze. And, as in Kulu, they have fenced new areas and declared them 'reserved forest'.

None of the reasons for the Gaddis' winter anxiety is new:

183

it is simply that during this century they have intensified. The most serious – from everyone's point of view – is the population explosion. Though the area we were walking through might, to the casual eye, have seemed empty waste land, it was not. There were villages, and the dusty stubbly patches were meant to be their wheat fields. Among the berberis bushes there were herds of skinny cattle and goats, and tethered outside houses there were buffalo. The population of Kangra is said to have increased by 73 per cent between 1891 and 1971, and by 1991 it will have doubled. As a result more and more land, previously available for grazing, is being cleared for cultivation. More people obviously also means more draught cattle and more milk cows and goats.

The Forest Department and the ecologists like to attribute the current 'ecological deterioration' to the transhumant flocks; and particularly to the goats. It was for this reason that flock sizes were 'frozen' in the 1970s. Since then shepherds have been obliged to restrict flocks to within the numbers stated in their permits.[4] And the keeping of goats is discouraged: for every goat given up, two sheep are allowed.

The blame for the increased pressure on grazing should not be landed on the Gaddis alone. The reason it is is political. Hans Bormann's brief was to take the migratory shepherds to task, but he saw that the government wanted unfairly to make a scapegoat of them. He saw that there had been a significant increase in the number of domestic sheep and goats and a massive increase, 81 per cent, in the number of cattle and buffalo in the area during the previous twenty years. Though some fodder crops are specially grown for cattle, he still considered that they represented the main 'grazing factor'.[5] And he went on to say:

'The migratory livestock holders cannot alone be blamed for the deterioration of the environment in H.P. [Himachal Pradesh]. A careful look has to be taken into the question of who else might be disturbingly involved in the cycles of nature.

'A policy which is formulated to restrict grazing has to apply to all graziers, i.e. to local cattle, buffaloes and goat holders as well. A policy which leaves the main cause for the ecological stress, but concentrates on a small group is only in search for scapegoats and will not in the long run succeed.

'Control of migratory graziers must include all graziers and must apply to all sections of graziers equally – irrespective of *political influence* [my italics].'[6]

The official lip-service paid to an anti-goat policy glosses over the real issue – there is a political motive for this. Delegates at conferences concerned with the protection of forests are enthusiastically anti-goat. Villages and forest guards are readily 'anti' the migratory flocks: the latter move on, so can be blamed for any damage without fear of their taking revenge. But the numbers of goats have already decreased by over 40 per cent during the last fifty years, and the terrain continues to deteriorate. It is not just because of the migratory flocks. The vast increase in domestic animals is indeed also 'disturbingly involved in the cycles of nature', as Bormann put it. But the point is that their owners represent many more votes than do the migratory flock-owners. A flock-owning family with, say, eighty animals represents only three or four voters. A household which owns, say, ten cattle and goats represents four or five voters. Restrictions and taxes on domestic stock would antagonize more voters than do restrictions on migratory flock-owners. A politician's concern for the environment is less ardent than his concern for his own popularity on polling day.

After walking eight or nine miles we were all despondent. Tchering was bad-tempered. Soban, still in his white tweed jacket, had spent the afternoon wrapped in a blanket on the niece's back, and was scarlet and feverish. The niece was exhausted. And we were all thirsty. I do not know how many people had been asked: 'Have you seen Munshi Ram's flock? There are two children with it, the boy is a little bigger than this one. No, there are no ponies. They are from Holi side.'

The questions and answers were in Kangri but by their endless repetition I could understand the gist of them.

The last people we had asked, some muleteers, had unconvincingly directed us back down a track we had come up. Then we were to go up through the wood, along a crest to a village, down to cross a ravine and up again. The village was full of ugly, hostile dogs and unusually offensive people. They sniggered as we walked through, and laughed openly when we took the wrong track down into the ravine. Sunni Devi was indignant.

'Where we come from, if any visitor comes to the village we say, "Come, sit down, have some tea." Or at least we offer water. What sort of people are these who don't know how to behave?'

The climb up from the ravine was very steep and unpleasant, and particularly dense with berberis bushes. As we reached the top, we could make out a flock among the berberis on the opposite hill, and against the rays of the sinking sun stood the unmistakable silhouette of a kilted Gaddi. My spirits rose. Sunni Devi began a conversation with the shepherd. Tchering took the opportunity to sleep. I sank, gingerly, on to the prickly ground.

No, it could not be described as a conversation. The shepherd was half a mile away; after every third or fourth word the caller had to pause, allowing time for the sound to carry, so that one phrase was clear of the next. To the unaccustomed ear it seems inconceivable that callers so far from each other, and projecting their voices with their utmost strength, can exchange information. The protagonists cannot make inter-jections; it is like a conversation on a one-way radio – one caller must switch off before the other can answer. The kilted silhouette emphasized his points with sweeping arm signals. It seemed to me that many words never reached their destina-tion, but were swept away by the air currents. To master the technique you must have to practise from childhood; calling to friends on the opposite side of the valley, or to a sister cow-herd away down the hill. When Sunni Devi joined us, a little breathless, I could see the exchange of information had not been encouraging. She said nothing and I did not ask what she had been told.

At the village at the top of the hill, the home of the old woman who had come with us all the way from the river, we were hospitably offered *charpois* to rest on. Now Sunni Devi let it be known that the kilted silhouette had seen our flock and shepherds a couple of days before. He thought they had been heading away, down the valley, but he was not sure. The villagers said that recently they had been camping in the fields here, but had since moved on. Dusk was not far off. Our elderly companion suggested, unenthusiastically, that we might stay for the night.

We lacked direction and determination. Sunni Devi was at the end of her tether. Tchering, restored after his sleep – or maybe it was just a resurgence of his usual concern for others – took pity on Sunni Devi; he was embarrassed by the exertion and inconvenience we had caused her. He took control, found a youth who had a theory as to where the shepherds might be and led us across half a mile of broken, uninviting ground. We were to turn left when we came out on a track and ask at a shop a hundred yards down on the right. We found a house on the right, though it did not look like a shop. We propped our tired bodies against a wall: the niece went in to ask.

'Yes, they are here! Up in the fields just above, but first come in and have some tea.' We sank on to *charpois* and gulped the tea, while the hostess picked all the broad beans in her patch of garden for us. And over the stile came Sunni Devi's husband. They did not even greet each other; he shook my hand, and Soban suddenly came back to life.

The camp was in a field of failed wheat. The owner had considered the benefit of the folded flock manuring it preferable to an attempt to preserve the crop. There had been little rain. Hot air from the plains hitting the cold air over the Dhaula Dhar causes thunderstorms there, but here clouds and minor air disturbances move freely overhead: the average rainfall is 50 inches – half Palampur's figure. The fresh snow that had fallen on the Dhaula Dhar the previous night had not benefited the dry southern ridges of the Sivaliks; the shepherds were praying for rain. The subsoil is so shallow here that it quickly dries out; even the shrubs were putting out no new shoots.

As Sunni Devi's guests our base was at the hearth used by her husband and her younger brother.

But we were also made to feel welcome at her elder brother's, Munshi Ram's, hearth; it was on the other side of the field, the far side of where the sheep were folded. His companions were a seventeen-year-old girl, elder sister to the niece who had come with us, and a twelve-year-old son, Renu (the eldest son was the Hamirpur student with the watch). Renu and Soban had greeted each other with the joy of old playmates. They upturned the basket that imprisoned the youngest lambs and kids, and all evening, using the stubble field as their sportsground, they jumped and cavorted like kids themselves.

Munshi Ram was not only the eldest, he was unquestionably the leader of the group. A school education or experience of an Outward Bound course are not the only ways of developing leadership qualities, whether they are needed to face the dangers of the mountainside, or to cope in a novel social

188

situation. Munshi Ram had never met me before; had probably never come face to face with a white woman – certainly not as a guest at his camp. I had walked over to where he had been bringing the flock slowly back towards camp, letting them have a final feed at the *adhotada* hedges before being folded for the night. In the diminishing light, just before dusk, everything was pale yellow. In the far distance the Dhaula Dhar looked like a transparent yellow film; I would not have noticed it if I had not known it was there. Munshi Ram came towards me, grasped my hand in his, sat me down on the ground and gave me a *biri*. It was not that he looked different from the two others – he was spare, with sturdy, muscular legs, and had a slightly grizzled stubble for a beard. But there was a difference in his bearing; the others might be indifferent to a predicament, but Munshi Ram would master it.

He called to Renu to stop playing and come and watch the flock while he walked me across to his hearth. He uncovered the utensils and sacks of grain and wool – the camp baggage which had been neatly stacked under blankets during the day – spread a blanket for me and told his daughter to light the fire while he went to milk a goat for the tea.

'We are happy that you come here to us. It is an honour. I know you are a friend of my sister's. But what do you eat? If we were at home it would be different; here we have nothing to offer you. Can you drink goat's milk? They can bring buffalo milk from the village, and *lassi*, too. And how will you sleep? I will bring a *charpoi* from the village; I have friends there and it isn't far.'

I had difficulty in dissuading him from bringing the *charpoi*: I had a disconcerting picture of myself perched up on a bed in the middle of an open field. I would much rather sleep inconspicuously on the ground. The villagers did bring buffalo milk and *lassi*, and later Munshi Ram arrived out of the darkness with his arms full of special fine, straight twigs for my mattress; for their own use Renu had cut a few irregular green branches.

Sunni Devi had sent her husband on an extravagant shopping expedition. He returned with a goatskin sack filled with tea, cooking fat, onions, wheat flour, packets of expensive spices and dal. She had been preparing the broad beans. Most people make a cooking hearth by carefully setting three stones to balance the pot; Gaddis rest the pots, very precariously, directly on the logs or twigs. The vessels have no handles; if they did, they would be awkward to carry, and would break when packed in the goat-hair string bags they use. Sunni Devi moved the pots on and off the fire with dexterity, using a pair of tongs – not the dainty ones used to arrange charcoal in a hookah, but more like a pair of elongated pliers. As she did so she showed off the finely drawn tattoo patterns on the backs of her hands.

'Do you like the *lassi* raw or fried? Will you eat rice, wheat chapattis or *makki ki roti*?'

'Whatever is easiest.'

'It is as you would like.'

I chose the maize bread, partly because I knew they valued the wheat flour and rice and could save them for another special occasion, but more because I like *makki ki roti*; they were a treat for me, as they are difficult to make, and in most households frowned on.

We were given deep iron dishes to wash in, which were then rinsed out and used to eat from. We were served first; then Sunni Devi's husband and her younger brother and lastly Soban (who had to be woken, as he was curled up asleep under a pile of blankets). Munshi Ram, his daughters and Renu ate at their own hearth, but they joined us afterwards at ours.

We sat round the fire well into the night. Though we were only at 2000 feet, it was cold and the glow from the warm embers was a pleasure. Shepherds and their families do not have the shelter of a dwelling at their winter pastures, only the protection of their blankets; it must be as cold and dismal here during a period of winter rain as it would be at 14,000 feet in July.

We talked of sheep and wool prices, here and in Scotland, as we shared the bottle of whisky we had brought, and were warmed from the inside as well as by the fire. Sunni Devi took a drop or two herself. Her husband threw it neat down his gullet, but did not become any more communicative. From time to time she had hinted at her lack of enthusiasm for life; and I remembered her comments to me in Deori about his fondness for spending money on *arak*. I wondered whether her underlying sadness was because she was disappointed in him and his lack of forcefulness. Perhaps the contrast with her elder brother made it worse; for Munshi Ram had confidence, owned twice the number of sheep and goats, and recently had acquired land in Kangra. And why was her husband, an in-law, sharing her brothers' grazing? She must have been married into a family with no grazing rights; maybe one that did not even have a flock. It looked as though she and her husband were being supported by the generosity of her own family. I did not want to ask her; to embarrass her by making her have to express her shame at the inadequacy of her in-laws.

Her younger brother did contribute a few comments to the conversation, while he spun by firelight, letting the *takli* drop as he did so into an iron dish, so that the wool would not gather dust, straw and thorns from the ground. But it was mostly Munshi Ram who talked.

'Our life is a bad one. [He used the word *ganda*, which literally means "dirty".] We eat bad food, drink bad water, and sometimes must camp in bad places. That's why those who have done their studies don't want to live this life. No wonder: it breaks your back and you're always being abused. Here we have to watch the flock even at night. If any of them

191

get into the fields over there, that's the last we'll see of them: the villagers will lock them up. Down here we need the children to help us. They are useful to herd the flock in the day; you can't expect them to do it at night. No, they don't come with us up in the hills, not until they are fifteen or so – it's too dangerous and uncomfortable for children and women – we'd spend all our time looking after them. They are better at home looking after the fields.'

Eight merino ewes and two rams were introduced into Kangra in 1908. But it has been during the last two decades that the Indian government, in association with German and New Zealand projects, have subsidized and encouraged the breeding of imported merinos; in an effort to improve the native stock and the quality of the wool. A little merino blood is acceptable to the shepherds but I have yet to meet a flock-owner who is a merino enthusiast. Munshi Ram certainly was not: his moustaches bristled with scorn.

'All right, the wool is finer, but it's soft, not strong. At the winter clip there's nothing of it – it's all come off on the thorny bushes. And anyway, in the autumn, when there is more of it, a merino fleece weighs less than one from our own sheep and we get the same price for a kilo of wool whatever it's like. So what's the good to us? The officials tell us we should do this and we should do that. What do they know about sheep and goats and how we have to live? We are told we would get a permit for two sheep for every goat we give up. Who knows if you would get it, and who would be daft enough to try?'

Shepherds do not see their goats as destructive monsters. They are fond of them. Goats are offered as a sacrifice to the gods; their milk is considered good for health and is used to feed newborn lambs, because ewes in poor condition often have inadequate milk. They are valued for their good sense and sure-footedness on the mountainside; and for the noise they make when frightened – if a bear or a leopard gets among a flock at night, goats will make a noise and wake the shepherds or their dogs; sheep die silently. To this traditional attachment is added the more recent economic attraction. For the flock-owner meat prices have increased out of proportion to the raw wool price shepherds receive, and goats are a more useful source of mutton than sheep. Today the income from goats sold for meat is nearly the same as the total income from sheep combining both wool and meat.[7] When animals are sold for slaughter it is a seller's market: if the price is not good enough, the commodity can be moved, on its own legs, to where the price is better.

Flocks could be better managed: there could be fewer, more productive animals. Munshi Ram was amazed to learn that on hill farms in Argyll, we called a ewe of five or six years a cast ewe and sold her for slaughter, or down to the lowlands. Some of his were twelve or fourteen. Such elderly stock results in infertility and low lambing rates; so does poor condition – caused by inadequate pasture and weakening diseases. Foot and mouth disease does not kill – for the flocks have some resistance to it – so much as debilitate: the ewes and nannies do not conceive, or they abort.[8] The lambing rate[9] (the number of lambs or kids per hundred ewes at weaning time) is 65–75 per cent, near enough the same as in the West Highlands. But there is a difference. Our percentage at birth is over a hundred; the few infertile ewes being compensated for by twin births. Our losses more often occur between birth and weaning – owing to bad weather, foxes or no attendant shepherd. The Gaddis are such attentive shepherds that they lose few lambs after birth. If they could increase their birth rate, their weaning rate could be much higher than ours.

It was well past everyone's bedtime; we had long ago finished the bottle of whisky and consumed an extravagant quantity of fuel, for warmth and to give ourselves light and companionship. As our small circle began to break up I felt we were alone in the world: there was not a sight or sound of anyone else. Sunni Devi said, 'Will you come to Deori at *Sankrant* in *Asarha*? We have kept a goat for three years in the name of the *Devi*. If you come, we will make the sacrifice to *Mataji* this year. We would like you to be there. Please come.'

I was touched, quite overcome that they should think of me with such honour. Of course I wanted to be able to be there. 'In the name of which *Mataji*?' It was a silly question; I knew they would answer 'The *Mataji*' or 'Our *Devi*'. I said it partly because I was so overwhelmed I did not know what else to say. But it brought a remarkable answer.

'Her name is Barsalang; she is the big *Devi* at Lamu, near Delhi.'

'Why in her name?' I asked.

'Because she is so important to us.'

I lay at the side of the field on my mattress of special twigs, a little way away from the others, who lay round the hearth. My sleeping bag was covered with a check blanket and my head pillowed on a *dora*. I was excited. Had I found a real clue to the question of the Gaddis' original home? Did the importance of Devi Barsalang from Lamu prove the theory that the first immigrants to Bramour came from Thanesar, after the fall of the Gupta empire in the mid-seventh century AD? I remembered something I had forgotten: that one of the first references I had found to the Gaddis had mentioned the idea of their originating somewhere near there, and that there were still Gaddis there in the late nineteenth century who were buffalo people.[10] I went to sleep dreaming of one day making a pilgrimage to Barsalang with Sunni Devi and Munshi Ram.

I did not sleep much during my stay at the camp because

from time to time throughout the night someone (Munshi Ram or one of the two others who took the watches in turn) would dash across the field letting out grunts and muffled shouts; I suppose to air his rage with any of the flock who were attempting a midnight feast. But I was happy to be disturbed: it was a waste to be asleep and miss the pleasure of lying out there. I was sorry when, woken by the screech of a brain-fever bird, I opened my eyes and found it was dawn. Renu would grab a kid from under the imprisoning basket and let it run to nuzzle its handsome mother while he milked her (goats are milked from the back) for the morning tea. I would still be tucked into my sleeping bag, sipping the hot thick tea, while Munshi Ram grabbed two or three ewes to dose them with salt and mustard oil 'to give them warmth'.

I was brought water to wash in, though they had to carry it half a mile from the spring. By then the flock were desperate to be on the move; goats and sheep in ones and twos broke away and ran, head down, towards the nearest hedge. In Lahoul they had rested quietly on the rocks, waiting until ten or eleven o'clock, when the shepherds had cooked and eaten and were ready to set off for the day's grazing. Here they were grazed morning and evening, while midday was spent at camp. Perhaps the habit is as a result of the midday heat; more probably it is because the winter grazing is so scanty and the flock that much more hungry. Renu and his sister took them, sheep and goats together, up a hill of scrub jungle, at the top of which stood the ruins of a temple. Once out of the glade the flock were hidden by the *shisam*, the eucalyptus and the creepers.

Much to my shame I realized that as I had been taking photographs I had been cutting with my zoom lens any signs of the women's Punjabi clothes, or of plastic jerry cans, or tins of cooking fat bearing brand names. Onlookers like me too easily attribute a 'traditional' way of life and an ancient culture to the trappings of costume. Tribals who lack pride or a sense of identity, paid to dance for tourists in traditional dress, make the occasion a dismal pageant.

The eighty thousand Gaddis, hardly a noticeable minority among the seven hundred million Indians, have an unusual combination of advantages which enable them to be a successful group. They have a strong cultural and geographical identity, a history of opportunism, and a reasonably prosperous livelihood. If the nation, made up of so many diverse minorities, is not to slide into the nightmare of millions of demoralized and job-searching refugees who squat in shanty towns on the outskirts of big cities, while a few perform tribal dances in fancy dress, then groups like the Gaddis, who are capable of sustaining a productive livelihood, must be encouraged. They ought not to be harassed into selling the flocks that are the source of their productivity, nor humiliated. It can be no fun for a youth like the disgruntled Kapur Singh when a carful of fancily dressed Bombay tourists bellow, 'You're only fit for *charani*'. And I thought of a boy I met when he was home on holiday from college. Tugging his ear lobes to emphasize the intensity of his feeling, he said he would help with household chores – cooking, cleaning or anything, 'but *please* don't send me out to do *charani*'.

Lying on my bed of twigs, under a brilliant Milky Way – there was no moon to outshine it – I felt humbled by what I had learnt from the Gaddis; by their manners, their hospitality and their proud civility. Never had I been happier.

I sat forlornly on a bus heading south. The backcloth of the Dhaula Dhar became fainter and fainter, as though stage lights were imperceptibly dimming, until it hung in the sky only in my mind's eye. The jagged crenellations of the Sivaliks gave way to plains – the crumpled paper had been flattened out; pitched roofs gave way to flat; the bus driver roared no longer at flocks of milk-white goats and sheep but at camels and stupid buffalo drawing bulging carts of chaff wrapped in sackcloth.

1. Richard Evans, in his *Proposal*, estimates that spinning on a *takli*, a hand spindle, 100 to 150 grams of wool may be spun in an eight-hour day: on a *chakra* (spinning wheel) the spinner can double the quantity. So to spin enough for a large blanket it takes 160 hours on a *takli*, and 80 hours on a *chakra*. Most Gaddi households use both spinning methods, so a blanket takes an average of 120 spinning hours. Add 80 hours for carding, and 20 hours for weaving: a total of 220 hours from the raw wool to the finished blanket, though another few hours should be added for the finishing, sewing, washing and shrinking. Five kilos of raw wool are needed, as during the cleaning and carding it loses nearly half its weight. Raw wool costs 25 to 35 rupees per kilo. At an average of 30 rupees per kilo, enough for a blanket would be worth 150 rupees.

2. Peter Molnar, *The American Scientist*, Vol. 74, 1986.

3. 'No good sized patch of suitable wood or jungle will be found in the low hills to which some tenant does not resort in winter.' More than a hundred years ago, there were already disputes over the rights to the grazing runs. There were endless altercations as to who held a 'hereditary' right and who a 'customary' right (a right of use). It was too complicated even for Lyall's enthusiasm for solving the shepherds' problems and his determination to codify all complex issues. He admitted defeat: he failed to establish who did and who did not have rights to the winter *bans*. 'No entry in the village records will be found with regard to winter sheep runs, though certain families have undoubtedly distinct and definite rights of a kind in them. I have however had a return of these winter grazing runs compiled . . . which may be of some assistance in the case of disputes. It is, however, in no sense a settlement record, for I purposely refrained from attesting it, or for testing its accuracy except here and there in a cursory way. The rights of the persons claiming to be *warisi* (inheritors) of the runs, and of those who are associated with them (if the latter have any rights) are

in a loose, fluid, sort of state. I did not wish to strengthen or petrify them by bringing them to book.' J. B. Lyall, *Land Settlement Report, 1865–72*. At a later stage, with the help of Lyall's report, it was established who had the right to which runs.

4. In the Department's eyes this is a separate issue from whether or not they have a right to grazing: the shepherds seldom accept the distinction.

5. He suggested that every household should be permitted only a limited number of domestic animals, and that there ought to be a heavy tax on all animals which a farmer could not maintain on the fodder grown on his own land.

6. Hans Bormann, *Shepherding in the Dhaula Dar*.

7. I calculate the annual income from a flock of 150 consisting of 70 goats and 80 sheep to be roughly as follows: 17 per cent of the goats are sold for slaughter, yielding 4500 rupees; 10 per cent of the sheep are sold for slaughter, yielding 3000 rupees. The wool of 60 sheep clipped (approximately 1 kg per sheep per year) at 30 rupees a kilogram yields 1800 rupees. The total income from the sheep in this case would total 4800 rupees, against the income from the goats, which would total 4500 rupees.

8. Protective vaccination exists but it is not regularly available, is expensive and involves the logistical difficulty of getting the flock to a veterinary dispensary.

9. Given by the Animal Husbandry Manager of the Dhaula Dhar Project.

10. *A Glossary of Tribes and Castes of the Punjab*, ed. H. A. Rose.

After the Journey

Initially when I had the idea of writing about the Gaddis I imagined I would produce material for posterity – anthropological records for a *Disappearing World* archive. The more I learnt about them the clearer it became that the Gaddis are not a vanishing people; they are likely rather to survive into the twenty-first century.

And now that I have finished writing it is evident to me, and will have been to the reader, that I was not involved in anthropological research; what I had was a rare opportunity to get to know people whose life is utterly unlike most of ours.

This book is largely an account of the good time I had while doing so, but it would be unfair if I did not add to it some conclusions from my year's journey. I would feel I had been unjust to the Gaddis if, having taken my pleasure, I made no attempt to offer some serious thoughts about their future.

I have explained that I do not give much credence to Bormann's opinion that many of the shepherds are willing to throw away their shepherd's crooks. I dispute his assessment of the chances of persuading them to give up shepherding not because I imagine that they are romantically devoted to their hardy, self-contained life; nor because I believe that they are

199

constrained by their *dharma*, though I do think that they give their Shiva-given calling and its associated cultural ties more significance than Bormann's cavalier dismissal implies. I dispute it because, as I see it, the income from their flocks is increasing, and has the potential to go on increasing. At the moment the greater part of that increase is derived from the officially despised goats. For that reason I cannot believe that the government's present efforts to restrict goat numbers will be a success. Changes in livestock holdings are unlikely to result from legislation: changes are more likely to happen as a consequence of economic incentives. The contemporary popularity of goats with the shepherds is partly because of the goats' ability to thrive on poor grazing. But it is also because at the moment they produce a better cash return than sheep. During the last ten or fifteen years the demand for meat, and therefore its price, has accelerated faster than the price of wool, so goats, more useful producers of meat than sheep, have become more financially attractive.

Even supposing that shepherds recognize the goats' detrimental effect on the environment, they would be unlikely to take any action: to make a sacrifice for the benefit of grandsons yet unborn is to them a meaningless concept. In their view (and the chances are that it is the realistic one) the benefit of the sacrifice would be reaped by someone else. If the government and the ecologists really want to see a shift away from goats and towards sheep, they should make every effort to boost the comparatively depressed value of sheep. They should subsidize a more appropriate breed – perhaps the hardy, dual-purpose hill cheviot – rather than the disparaged park merino. And they should look into the wool dealers' monopoly of the industry and innovate a scheme encouraging a good price for the better-quality wool: it would be an incentive for shepherds to produce good, long-stapled fleeces.

These are some of the approaches that could make sheep

more profitable. But there is another possible development to be explored. If Gaddi households were able to process more of their own wool they could improve their annual income from it and would immediately appreciate the encouragement towards sheep-breeding. Simple 'cottage' machinery should be devised and introduced – plant machinery is unlikely to benefit an industry which is so tied to the home and revolves round domestic chores – so that they can card and spin more wool. At the moment, because shepherds' families do not have the time to process more than a small proportion of their wool, they sell it raw to the dealers. It is the latter, as well as the Punjabi mill-owners who manufacture it, who make the fat profit.

I believe the government's anti-goat policy would be more likely to succeed if, rather than vainly attempting to restrict goat numbers, it turned its attention to encouraging wool production from sheep. But it would have to be careful to stimulate it in a way which ensured that the benefit went to the wool-producers themselves. Policy-makers ought to try to create a situation where flock-owners *want* to breed sheep rather than goats. They need not be too anxious about creating a market for the wool: it already exists. Middle-class Indians' demand for a variety of woollen goods is expanding almost as fast as their appetite for meat (which is why India has begun to import wool from Australia), but at the moment the wool-growers themselves are not benefiting from the situation. Exports of quality hand-spun and hand-woven articles could also be a useful earner of foreign exchange. While concentrating on the importance of the wool industry, it should not be forgotten that sheep are perfectly good meat animals, provided they have adequate grazing. It is true, though, that the Gaddis' sheep would be improved by the introduction of some new blood, preferably dual-purpose stock.

*

I began to write this book in a hay-shed in India. It was difficult: everything was too familiar and too diffuse. I felt strangled by the effort of trying to qualify everything I wrote. In India every statement bears so many alternative meanings and interpretations.

In the end I wrote most of it in London. When I read through what I had written, it seemed too easy, too distilled and too romantic. I remembered a phrase from Wordsworth's Preface to *Lyrical Ballads* that I had not thought of since I was a student: 'emotion recollected in tranquillity'.

The emotion, he said, is contemplated until 'the tranquillity gradually disappears, and an emotion, kindred to that which was before the subject of contemplation, is gradually produced, and does itself actually exist in the mind.'

My memory of Wordsworth's work was that, for all the theory of describing only what was 'natural', the result was contrived. Had I done the same? Did anything I had seen or learnt or felt really exist as I have presented it?

The journey had turned out to be a stretching, an expansion of my own experience. Sometimes as I wrote, envisaging a length of the path, a view or an evening among friends, I was misty-eyed and felt that constriction at the bottom of the rib cage when it feels too small to hold all your breath. Time spent in the Himalayas, even the memory of particular moments there, can be very moving; they are so beautiful, and so close to the gods perhaps.

Have I written a fantasy contrived for my pleasure? If so, the Gaddis should not be blamed. Their setting and the idea of their migration is romantic, and for me many incidents on the journey have become romantic stories, but my portrayal of the Gaddis ought not to be coloured by subjective romanticism. Of course there are old men who enjoy indulging themselves in recalling the good old days when every man owned a huge flock and grass grew green and lush everywhere, but on the whole Gaddis do not indulge in the wingeing gloom of people whose role is drawing to an end.

They have a good chance of not being crystallized into museum exhibits. They are a people who have retained their cultural identity and traditional livelihood (and appearance) while making their way towards the next century. Many Gaddis have the zest to deal with the changing world. The Manali vet told me how a number of shepherds recently conquered epidemics of a sudden lethal pneumonia in their flocks by themselves learning to administer antibiotic injections. I had noticed discarded phials at campsites away up on the hillsides and wondered who had used them and for what. Whether they succeed in the future will in part depend on the wisdom of the policy instigators and executives; as well as on their adopting a more honest and less political approach to all causes of environmental damage.

Loss of cultural identity should not be a necessary corollary to being a success in the contemporary world. Civil servants, politicians and schoolteachers – instigators of social attitudes – might remember that one of India's adages is 'Unity in Diversity'. Essential for a sense of well-being is a feeling of pride in what you do and who you are. A young Gaddi may feel proud to wear a new, very black, *dora*; he may feel reassured to know that others can recognize his identity. And those who made it may enjoy the satisfaction of being good *dora*-makers; their skill may contribute to their own sense of well-being. But the feeling can easily be turned inside out. Self-confidence is shattered if you are made ashamed of your family, your livelihood, or what you wear. Your *dora* will not bolster you if your college classmates mock your shepherding background. Indian society is as stratified as ever but the old acceptance of that stratification is being tarnished by a new snobbery. Recently I was waiting in Hamirpur bus stand in Kangra. Hundreds of youths had just come out of the Government College. They strutted about in trainers and crotch-hugging 'terry-cot' trousers, self-consciously adjusting their tailored shirts. I wondered if Sunni Devi's nephew (Munshi Ram's eldest son, the guardian of the watch) was among the crowd.

I feel that the Gaddis of the Budil valley suffer from a certain sense of shame and embarrassment; Gaddis of the Ravi valley and Kangra much less so. I am sure it is linked with the prosperity of the latter. Prosperity is crucial to pride and the sense of well-being. Flock-owning Gaddis have been able to acquire more land in Kangra during the last twenty-five years than Kangra people themselves.[1] That gives them pride and re-assurance. It is particularly important when it comes to marrying their daughters.

If Sunni Devi does manage to buy land in Kangra, her family will be in an enviable position when it is time for Munni to be married.

1. P. R. Phillimore, 'Marriage and Social Organisation among Pastoralists of the Dhaula Dhar'.

Glossary

arak locally distilled liquor

Asarha Indian calendar month, corresponding to September/October

Ayurvedic (medicine) traditional Indian system of medicine

ban grazing run on the winter pastures

batti agent or shop

Bhadon Indian calendar month, corresponding to August/September

bhana cymbal

bhut ghost or spirit

biri small cigarette: tobacco rolled inside a leaf

chakra spinning wheel

chang local beer, brewed from rice or barley

charani herding; often pejorative in common usage

charas cannabis; the resin is smoked mixed with tobacco

charpoi wooden bedstead frame on legs, woven across with webbing or string

chaukidar caretaker or guard

Chaurasi name of the main square at Bramour: 'eighty-four'

chela devotee or medium of a deity

chilam the bowl of a hookah, often used instead of the complete apparatus while on the move

chola the cloak traditionally worn by Gaddi men

chulha cooking hearth: either a fire set on the ground, or a hearth built with stones or clay

dai midwife

dal (rajma; ma; chole; masoor) pulses

darshan sight or experience

deodar *Cedrus deodara*: Himalayan cedar

devi (deviji) deity

devta (deota) female deity

dhar ridge; also a grazing ground in Kangra and Gadderan

dharm-behin adopted sister

dharm-bhai adopted brother

dharma life's duty or purpose

dora black wool rope, worn round the waist by Gaddi men, women and children

gahar grazing grounds en route

galu a pass: a neck between rocks or mountains

Gayatri a prayer, recited by Brahmins

ghi clarified butter

gompa Buddhist monastery or temple

got grazing ground in Gadderan and Kulu

gur raw sugar

halwa a sweetmeat

jangli wild, ignorant; of the jungle

jelebi a sweetmeat

jhula a swing: here, a bridge with a box pulley

jot a saddle-shaped pass

jutha that which has been touched by another and will therefore pollute; usually though not always refers to food, drink or something to be smoked

karnal a land measurement; a tenth of an acre in Kangra

Khampa a trading community, originally from Tibet

khana (pakka khana; kacca khana) food (cooked food; raw food)

kurhi a sauce made from yoghurt
kurta a long shirt, worn outside pyjamas
kuth a root crop, valued for medicine

lassi buttermilk
lingam phallic symbol of Lord Shiva
luanchari the long, full dress worn by Gaddini

mat
morar }names of particular grasses
Mataji mother; with the '-ji' ending as here shows familiar respect; often refers to the female deity

nala valley or river
namaste the usual greeting
nautor land given to the landless (and the policy of giving it)
niru a grass; from *nira*, meaning blue

pahari of the hills
pakora fried snack – vegetable in batter
panda priest
pangat the order, or grouping, of seating in lines on the ground at a marriage or other ceremony
paratha unleavened bread, fried
pashmina 'cashmere' wool: the undercoat of a breed of goat only produced when the animals are living at a high altitude
patwari village accountant and record-keeper
pradhan village headman
prasad an edible offering to a deity, which is subsequently offered to other people
puja religious ceremony; prayer
pujari a deity's officiating priest

'Ram Ram'; *'thik thak'* a rural greeting and its answer
renuka tinder box
rishi renowned holy man

Sankrant a phase in the moon's cycle
sarpanch head of a village council
sattu parched barley ground into flour
shisham tree, with valued hard timber
Shivji familiar name for Lord Shiva

tach grazing ground, in Kulu and Gadderan
takli hand spindle
tawa a girdle; flat iron dish used for making chapattis
tehsil administrative division; part of a named district
tejbuta wild-growing medicinal root
thakur baron, or Rajput dignitary (a title many assume)
thali metal plate with a raised lip
thang grazing ground, in Lahoul
tika mark on forehead
tol a measure; in this case forty
trishul trident
tulsi basil

vaidya one who has knowledge of and practises Ayurvedic medicine

yagya a formal Hindu ceremony
yoni symbolical female genitals

Bibliography

Barnes, G. C. and Lyall, J. B., *Report of the Land Revenue Settlement of the Kangra District, Punjab*, Lahore, 1889

Basham, A. L., *The Wonder That Was India*, London, 1967

Bormann, Hans-Herbert, 'Shepherding in the Dhaula Dhar': A Report on behalf of the Indo-German Integrated Farm Forestry Project 'Dhaula Dhar', 1980

Bose, Nirmal Kumar, *Some Indian Tribes*, Delhi, 1973 ('The Gaddi', pp. 83–100)

Evans, Richard, *A Proposal to develop improved woollen textiles in the cottage sector in services*, Himachal Pradesh, 1983

Furer-Haimendorf, Christoph von, *Himalayan Traders*, London, 1975

Furer-Haimendorf, Christoph von, *A Himalayan Tribe: From Cattle to Cash*, Delhi, 1980

Goetz, H., *Early Wooden Temples of Chamba*, Leiden, 1955

Grierson, Sir G. A., *Linguistic Survey of India*, Calcutta, 1916 (reprinted Delhi, 1967)

Hutchinson J. and Vogel, J. P. H., *History of the Punjab Hill States* (2 vols.), Lahore, 1933

Ibbetson, Sir Denzil, *Punjab Castes*, Lahore, 1916

Kayastha, S. L., *The Himalayan Beas Basin: A Study in Habitat, Economy and Society*, Benares, 1964

Lyall, J. B., *Report of the Land Settlement of the Kangra District, Punjab, 1865–72*, Lahore, 1876

Negi, T. S., *Scheduled Tribes of Himachal Pradesh: A Profile*, Delhi (privately published), 1976

O'Brien, E. and Morris, M., *The Kangra Gaddis*, Punjab Ethnography No. 2, Lahore, 1900

Parry, J. P., *Caste and Kinship in Kangra*, London, 1979

Phillimore, Peter R., 'Marriage and Social Organisation among Pastoralists of the Dhaula Dhar', thesis presented for D.Phil, Department of Anthropology, University of Durham, 1982

Phillimorę, Peter R., 'Transhumance and Environmental Damage', paper presented to the 7th European Conference of Modern South Asian Studies, London University, 1981

Randhawa, M. S., *Travels in the Western Himalayas*, Delhi, 1974

Rose, H. A. (ed.), *A Glossary of Tribes and Castes of the Punjab Vol. II*, Lahore, 1911

Shashi, S. S., *The Gaddi Tribe of Himachal Pradesh*, Delhi, 1977

Shashi, S. S., *The Shepherds of India*, Delhi, 1978

Newell, William H., 'An Upper Ravi Village: The Process of Change in Himachal Pradesh', from *Change and Continuity in India's Villages*, ed. K. Ishwaran, Columbia, 1970

Newell, William H., 'Goshani, a Gaddi Village in the Himalayas', from *India's Villages*, ed. N. Srinivas, Bombay, 1960

Newell, William H., *Census of India 1961*, Vol. XX, Part V-B: 'The Scheduled Castes and Tribes of the Brahmaur Tahsil of Chamba District', Simla, 1967

Newell, William H., 'Intercaste Marriages in Kugti Villages', *MAN* Vol. 63, no. 59, 1963

Singh, Ram Chandra Pal (ed.), *Census of India 1961*, Vol. XX, *Himachal Pradesh* Part VI, Village Surveys no. 5, Brahmaur

Punjab District Gazetteer 1906, Vol X-A. *Kangra District* Part A, Civil and Military Gazette Press, Lahore

Punjab State Gazetteer 1910, Vol XXII-A, *Chamba State*, Civil and Military Gazette Press, Lahore

Punjab District Gazetteer 1918, Vol XXX-A, *Kangra District* Part III (Lahoul), Government Printing, Lahore

Gazetteer of Mandi State 1904, Civil and Military Gazette Press, Lahore

6)

P I R

CHAMBA ■

Ravi River

DHAULA

Karamukh ••• Budil Ri

BRAMOUR ■ •••

Dhan

Ravi

Mani
13,000 ft

DHARAMSALA ■

Holi •
Riv

Il
Kha
Pas
16,72•

Nayag

PATHANKOT
□

PALAMPUR
■

KANGRA

BAIJN

JO

HIMACHAL
PRADESH

INDIA

DERA
GOPIPUR
□

JAWALAMUKHI
■

Beas River